THE DARK REHAB

Tarik Balkan

First published by Busybird Publishing 2025

Copyright © 2025 Tarik Balkan

ISBN:
Print: 978-1-923216-74-7

This work is copyright. Apart from any use permitted under the Copyright Act 1968, no part of this publication may be reproduced, stored in a retrieval system or transmitted in any form or by any means, electronic, mechanical, photocopying, recording or otherwise, without the prior written permission of Tarik Balkan.

The information in this book is based on the author's experiences and opinions. The author and publisher disclaim responsibility for any adverse consequences, which may result from use of the information contained herein. Permission to use any external content has been sought by the author. Any breaches will be rectified in further editions of the book.

Cover Image: Pixabay

Cover design: Busybird Publishing

Layout and typesetting: Busybird Publishing

Busybird Publishing
2/118 Para Road
Montmorency, Victoria
Australia 3094
www.busybird.com.au

The contents of this book may have some adverse affect on some people which I can understand, however promulgating my emotions in the darkest moments of my life in the past six years is not about pointing a finger at anyone.

We're constantly told that statistically we're not alone but no one knows that we're doing it alone, so this book is about awareness as we don't want to be misheard, misunderstood and ignored, so therefore if I offend or upset any one with the contents of this book, I sincerely apologise.

In the darkest days, hours and
minutes of our lives there can be
a light at the end of our tunnel,
for some of us we may be lucky
enough to see it and reach for it,
unfortunately not for all.

Tarik Balkan

Chapter 1

On early July 2008 I started to work in a well known and well established company in the western suburbs of Melbourne. Me, personally being well established in the mature department and with my dignified attitude towards my future and my diligent, punctual and respectful attitude towards my employment I seem to have fitted in quite well, with these valuable qualities within short period being with this company I was asked to become a team leader.

Being enticed with the prospect of receiving extra pay I had accepted the position quite gracefully and started to look forward to the challenges ahead with a positive attitude. However in saying all that I'm not trying to put myself on a pedestal. I'm just a hard working person trying to do my best to make life as comfortable as it is humanly possible for my family.

Anyhow it really was a great beginning, being excepted by six of my new team members, so the weeks turning into months, months turning into years by now everything is working out really good, plenty of work plenty of overtime that has helped my financial situation immensely. While this is all going great. the afternoon team leader decided to come to dayshift with me to be my second in charge but he just couldn't except the fact of me being his team leader, maybe he had an issue with nationality differences, but with me being older and understanding I've excepted the way he was, even though he was undermining me and totally disrespecting me I somehow took him under my wing so there's no problem. I guess I didn't want him to get in trouble with our managers.

So as the time gone by I am humbly excepting the fact that in the eyes and the opinions of managers I am developing a reputation of being a hard worker, knowing that I except any challenge no job too big or too small, great feeling so as all this is going well I've been asked to attend some courses, one of them was health safety environment [HSE] master class for managers, load restraint "in depth" course, A few of three and a half hour forklift refresher courses and first aid course.

So early January two thousand and thirteen getting an order ready for one of our regular customers, it was all assorted twelve metres long pipes with various diameters, I prepared majority of the order, towards the completion of the order however one of the twelve meter by hundred and sixty millimetre pipe was dropped behind a crate, I've grabbed one end of the pipe with both hands trying get it out of where it was between the two crates in the way of manoeuvring it on to the tine's of the forklift, in doing that at the same time I was pulling the pipe towards myself, as this was happening my right hand slipped and let go of the pipe but my left hand did not let go of the pipe when it flung back, so it pulled and jolted my left arm and my left shoulder, this happened on Friday afternoon, did not pay much attention to it on the day. However the next day Saturday afternoon my left forearm and mainly my left shoulder started to become painful, late in the afternoon started to take painkillers, when came Sunday morning the pain especially on my left shoulder become so unbearable that I started to take stronger pain killers.

About mid morning on Sunday I've called my manager and explained the situation I'm in and informed him of what happened, his response was fantastic, he told me that he'll pick me up first thing Monday morning and take me to a clinic in Laverton north, and he did. Seen the doctor received some more strong pain killers and went home. Stayed home for about ten days and then went back to the clinic received some physiotherapy more pills and went back to work on light duties, and within days I was back on the forklift performing my usual pre injury tasks.

This went on until one day in April two thousand and thirteen approximately two fifteen in the afternoon one of the officials came up to me and told me that I cannot complete the task of loading the truck I was working on because I was on light duties and that if I wanted to do overtime I had to go back to see the doctor to get a clearance, so I did see the doctor to get the clearance so as far as my managers were concerned I was back to normal. So this is where it all begins.

Being on one wage and honouring my responsibilities both at home and at work, with or without pain killers at times I kept working, and about ten to twelve months later I've seen my family doctor about pain management mostly about my left shoulder, he send me to get x-rays for my shoulder, when the x-rays came back to my doctor he did give me some different pain killers and told me that I should get cortisone injection done on my left shoulder, I did arrange to get the injection and received it twice within six months. I found that there was no benefit from the cortisone injections at all, and then in the space of three years between two thousand and fourteen and two thousand seventeen I had Platelet rich plasma [PRP] injections done on both my left shoulder and my left elbow, where it did not help at all, in fact it really escalated the pain to an unbearable levels, the cost of the PRP was two hundred dollars per session, I've paid for the first session and my employer paid for the next two. However each time I've had the PRP sessions done I felt there was no follow up from my employer to see if I was okay, as always business as usual, as long as I'm on the fork lift leading the team, performing my usual tasks with or without pain, with or without pain killers it did not seem to matter, and there was no concern at all.

In the six years I've worked with this pain quite often I was asked why did I do it and why did I not do anything much sooner? Well as I mentioned before, honouring my responsibilities of leading my team performing my tasks to the best of my ability, and most importantly I never wanted to go on any work injury recovery plan with any of my employers in the past, I guess I was always afraid of disturbing the peace, and I was always worried that it might come to a point where my employment with the company may be compromised and I could be threatened with a termination of my employment. So bearing all that in mind I quite often felt that I had no other choice but to put my head down and keep working no matter what. This is the reason why I kept pushing with my injured shoulder and my injured left arm as long as I did for six long and agonizing years. Until early March two thousand and nineteen I found that I simply can't push anymore, by now the pain on my left shoulder and my left arm had become so unbearable that I realized I can't do this much more and that I had to do something about it.

Chapter 2

Well, this is where the real agony and a life changing experience begins, One day early March two thousand and nineteen I finally gave in and made the decision to go and see my occupational health and safety [OHS] manager to begin the procedures to repair my left shoulder and arm injuries, it was all good and excepted on professional grounds, we filled all the appropriate forms, signed them and send them to both the work injury department and the insurer.

We received a reply from both that my claim was excepted on the seventeenth of March twenty nineteen. Fantastic I instantly thought this is great with a bit of luck I will be free from all this pain I've been suffering for the last six years. Anyway while I'm all joyful about getting my injuries repaired exactly five days after receiving the acceptance of my injury claim the inevitable fear of mine had become a reality. For something so little and so unworthy I received a First and Final written warning. Well after working for this company for almost eleven years, working almost every Saturday and just about every public holiday, being diligent and always hard working and always being respectful towards authoritative figures of the company receiving the first and final warning had some terribly disturbing effect on my head in the way of thinking, concentrating and having a normal day in every aspect on what I do on day to day basis. This happened on the twenty second of March twenty nineteen.

I received a call to go to the front office to have a discussion about a mistake on the large truck I've loaded and the truck had left the premises, so the three senior officials called the truck driver to come back to the loading bay so we can rectify the situation, so when the truck came back to the loading bay and after inspecting the load yes we noticed that instead of twenty binders on the product the driver only used fourteen binders, knowing that I've personally instructed the driver to use twenty binders, by now the driver excepted the fault and the responsibility and he was very apologetic and remorseful but the drivers fault was totally ignored, so with the three senior officials we all went back to the front office again and me being remorsefully apologetic, explained that I've instructed the driver to do the right thing and use the binders safely and appropriately, and under no circumstances I've informed any of my officials that the truck was personally checked by me for safety before leaving the loading bay, well by one of the senior officials I was told it was fair enough but however they will have a further discussions with me some time next week.

Well I thought I've done my best to be remorseful and I apologized for something that definitely not a safety breach at all. Fair enough on the twenty sixth of March I was called in to OHS managers office together with distribution manager they both wanted to hear my side of what occurred on the twenty second of March.

Well yesterday and today being Tuesday the twenty sixth of March almost the end of my shift we sat down and I clearly and remorsefully explained exactly what had happened again and as a team leader I informed them that I'll make sure that it will not happen again not only to me but to any of my team members. So I don't know if it was a meeting or a gentle interrogation but I thought I handled myself very well, I thought I had nothing to lose. I did feel comfortable because there was no mention about a disciplinary action that was going to be presented to me the very next day.

Well sure enough the next day worked all day everything is going really well I thought, but to my surprise I was called into my manager's office just before the end of my shift wow !! how cunning is this, here he is asking me to sign a first and final written warning, so because I'm entering the first stages of my injury repairs and rehabilitation and this is going to be a big deal and a big let down to a certain official, that must become like a defeat that has made this person angry so that the minute I make a wrong move or a slight mistake that I'm out the door, how disrespectful, cunning and totally dishonest one would think. Just three months ago early January I received a gift from my manager a bottle of whisky telling me how great I'm doing my job and the loading bays are operating so smoothly, and two weeks before that for x mass I received another bottle of whisky same thing that he was very happy with the way I was operating. Anyway in receiving the written warning I was absolutely devastated, disappointed, I felt very hurt I just did not know how to react, what to think or what to do, I just went numb it really was quite unexplainable what and how I felt. I just told my manager that this was totally unfair and unacceptable and without signing the written warning I walked out of his office.

Driving home that afternoon I really don't know how I got home, there was this violently burning rage in my head, by this stage I'm in the back yard of my house, I can feel this is triggering high levels of stress, I feel that I'm going to lose my job after eleven years, I'm getting to old to start with a new company again, while this is going on in my head I can feel the anxiety levels rising too, instant feeling of uselessness starting to set in. Where do I go? What do I do? Do I hurt someone? Do I hurt myself? Oh boy these feelings are becoming so uncontrollable that I just don't know how to calm myself down.

So the next day twenty eighth of March Thursday I went to see my family doctor to get some help, firstly he gave me some more pain killers, after talking for about ten to fifteen minutes he gave me prescription for anti depressants [valdoxan 25mg] and [temazepam 10mg] and my GP informed me to call help line and he referred me to a psychologist. My first session with psychologist is on first of April twenty nineteen. After the session with my GP I've emailed my two day absent forms to my manager and returned home in a lot of pain both mentally and physically. After a few coffees and not knowing what to do, I decided to call the union official where I'm a member, the conversation was good I was referred to see a lawyer in the event if things gets out of control that I have a legal support.

Next three days day and night I just stayed home not only trying to manage my physical pain but at the same time trying to make some sense of the predicament I found myself in. I find myself trembling at times, thinking about myself being a tough guy a strong man yet I go into the back yard in a dark corner somewhere crying like a little boy, no one to hold me by the hand, no one putting their hand on my shoulder and telling me that everything is going to be alright. I don't know how to deal with this but one thing I know for sure is that I've entered into a cold, dark and a very lonely era in my life that I've never been before.

Chapter 3

Monday April 1, 2019.

Up about two am this morning lots of coffees and cigarettes, spending a lot of time outside in the dark, starring into the darkness and just thinking about my future, my physical ability and my mental stability, I'm finding it extremely hard that thinking about all the issues that goes around and around in my head is not getting me anywhere. Anyhow I've received my first counselling session this afternoon, what a waste of time and effort I thought, the lady I've seen spent the first twenty five minutes on trying to establish appropriate forms and how her company would have financial benefits from my sad situation. And then we started to have a chat, and every question I've answered the response was mmmmmm. Before I left she gave me some forms to fill, couple of the questions were, do I want to kill someone and do I want to commit suicide? Well she won't see me until the sixth of may, so in reality if I wanted to kill someone or decided to commit suicide I would have a whole month to do it. How pathetic, with this kind of attitude from the counselling session if anything I felt worse than before I've seen her.` not a very good start, again got back home with nothing to hold on to, not knowing what to think or even how to think.

April 2, 2019.

Up and out of bed at two thirty eight this morning, once again coffee and cigarettes unlimited, in the back yard in the dark, thinking of the same things over and over again, nowhere to go, no one to turn to, no one understands, no one cares and most importantly no one has the time, so you learn to stew in your own misery, no other choice. Seen the lawyer this morning, I guess she whispered a lot of sweet nothings in to my ear so I can be her client, the best thing about her taking my case on is that no win no fee I have explained my situation fully to her, I'll just have to wait and see how good and how far she'll support me?

April 3, 2019.

Seen the work injury doctor this morning, we starting to get into it now with my injury case, and I have a referral to see an orthopaedic surgeon for an independent assessment to see how real my injuries are, apparently this is a common practise, it doesn't matter how you feel about it just need to go along with it. The rest of the day and night is just a usual blur. Thinking and more thinking.

April 8, 2019.

Very early morning up and out of bed again, lots of coffees and cigarettes again. By now where ever I am, it sure is starting to feel too deep and too dark and starting to get too lonely, the most annoying thing about this brand new feelings and experiences that I'm going through is that when some people with no knowledge at all and haven't been where I am, telling me that everything is going to be alright, without them realizing it they are making me feel like I've been patronized, I can't help thinking that they must think that I'm mad or I'm an idiot or do they think that I've lost control over my emotions? So much is going through my head is that I feel I need to learn to live with it. I'm starting to find that twenty four hours in a day is a lot of hours to deal with all this, one of the painful issues about all this is trying to smile in the presence of my wife, I just don't want to give her any grief about my situation, I know she worries about me and I know she sheds lots of silent tears about me, she doesn't deserve any of my misery, just thinking about this is giving me more grief. Anyway all this feels like a story or a movie that I'm watching, once upon a time I was tough I was strong and in my own ways I felt unbeatable, but now down on my knees not knowing where this miserable journey is taking me? Yeah I am holding on but it's getting harder by the day.

April 10, 2019.
As usual up and early this morning in the back yard in the dark waiting for the beginning of a new day for no reason at all. It's the same thing with unlimited coffees and cigarettes again with the same misery. Seen the orthopaedic surgeon today for an independent medical examination, the report from him will go to work injury doctor and the insurer and then the decision will be made on when, where and which surgeon will perform the surgery on my left shoulder. Oh by the way no one's listening at the moment about my left forearm. Anyhow I get the feeling that medical football game has just began where I get handballed from one medical professional to another. Yeah quite often I wish that I didn't injure myself at work or that I was able to continue with a minimal pain until my retirement age that I didn't have to go through any of this at all. As you are reading this you've probably noticed that there are days missing on what I've been writing so far is that those are the days I don't feel like writing anything and I certainly don't want to associate with anyone, I just want to be left alone, I'm not in the mood to speak to anyone at all.

April 12, 2019.
Same again very early beginning again with unlimited coffees and cigarettes, talking about cigarettes, in the beginning of the year I've minimized the quantity from thirty cigarettes a day down to between ten to fifteen cigarettes per day with the idea that I'm getting older with that in mind I decided to pay more attention to my health and even stopped drinking alcohol, but now dealing with all these issues in my life where I feel there's no future I feel as if I'm letting go a lot of the quality values that meant the world to me, now good thing is that I still don't drink alcohol but the number of the cigarettes have gone up to sixty per day, and coffees I could have up to four in the first hour once I get out of bed, anyway I've seen the doctor again today for more pain killers because I seem to be taking a little excessively these days, and I'm trying to get another session with the psychologist only to find out that there's no appointment available until the sixth of may, too bad if I was

getting to the point of losing control, I'm hoping that I could hold on until then.

April 13, 2019.
Up and out of bed very early again, the effects of the pain killers are not lasting as long as they are suppose to so the minute I get out of bed I start taking pills before anything, again in the back yard in the dark with my coffee and my cigarettes as the best company I can have at the moment, and thinking of so many unimaginable things, but for now I'm a bit reluctant to put any of these thoughts on these pages at the moment, while I'm wiping my tears I'm thinking that if any one finds this diary the consequences are that my daily thoughts, feeling and the things that I do and might do could become hurtful and maybe even offensive to some people, so for the moment I just don't have the time, strength or the patience, I just need to sit here in silence and deal with it the best way I can. And at the same time I can't help but think that there are a lot of stormy days and a lot of rocky roads ahead, so I'm trying to hold onto whatever the patience I have left, and as usual the rest of the day complete silence, just waiting for medical appointments to get my injuries repaired so I can get my life back in order again.

April 18, 2019.
Today I have an appointment for MRI scan done on my left shoulder and trying to get an approval for this from the insurance company was like pulling somebody's tooth out, it definitely wasn't easy to convince the case manager of the insurer that this was urgent, another appointment for MRI could be a month away. Any way throughout the day with so many phone calls with doctors and the case manager from the insurer that I was asked to make an appointment to see a physio, I think that a physiotherapy sessions might repair my injured left shoulder is what they might be thinking, at the same time I'm trying to tell them about my left forearm, but no one is listening or acknowledging that it is painful and that it needs attention, it truly feels like I'm talking to myself and this is really getting annoying that I'm been ignored about my

left forearm, so by now late afternoon all this is really escalating the stress levels to the highest point. I'm finding that I simply can't talk to anyone, I just don't need anyone's sarcasm or useless inputs, for some reason when people talk to me with no knowledge and no understanding of what I'm going through and what I'm dealing with not only it's annoying but it is antagonizing as well, so another useless day and angry day, I just feel the need to do something, some very powerful thoughts are going through in my head, it feels I'm not in control any more, I'm lost I don't know where I am and I don't know what to do, it really feels scary, very heavy breathing at the moment, it certainly feels like the end is near, I'm scared and the tears are rolling down my face uncontrollably and I find myself trembling with rage.

Chapter
4

April 19, 2019.
I'm writing about today very late at night, Today was the darkest day of my life, I've never felt like this before, I almost put an end to it all, because I'm writing about this today doesn't mean that I'm bragging or proud of it, far from it. So here we go, as usual up and early very early this morning out in the back yard in my usual spot with my coffee and my cigarettes, staring in to the emptiness feeling absolutely blank, with the idea that there's no way out of this, there's no solution and there's no way any of this is going to be resolved, there's this powerful feeling, it felt as if I was hearing voices in my head to let go and give up, it felt as if I was pinned against a brick wall.

Okay now after hearing the voices in my head my attention turned into an area where I never thought I would find myself in this direction, but some invisible yet so powerful feeling was pushing me towards this direction, however I found no reluctance but to complete this absolutely forbidden task, in all my years I've always thought that this was a useless task, I've always thought that this kind of behaviour was granted to silly people, I've always thought that even contemplating this kind of act puts you into the category of idiotic people, well I don't know if I was wrong all those years about my personalized opinions or am I wrong now that I'm contemplating the unimaginable, a bit confusing I feel, but for some reason I feel the need to go through with it, and put an end to this misery for good!

Oh by the way it is late September two thousand and twenty now that I'm writing about this is because it's only now that I've built up enough courage and gathered some valuable information about suicide through communicating with some people who have been there. I am reluctant writing about all this but I'm hopeful that it may help some people some day, The almost final moments of my life and the almost final action of my life has never been shared with anyone before until now. So here it goes, on that dark, lonely and with no way out of it all feeling day I've decided to work out a plan, a plan of action that will end it all, so I started thinking about it from about two am that morning, I didn't want to jump off a bridge, I didn't want to pull the trigger, I thought it might legally get messy for my family, I didn't want my family to have financial burden at the time of loosing me, so I thought I've came up with a really good plan, a plan that I'll have an accident with my ute and it will be all over without any suspicion at all.

Okay the time has come, I've found a perfect spot where it is a bit hilly, the heavy quarry trucks rolling down the hill with the speed of up to one hundred kilometres an hour, when the truck comes down to the bottom of the hill and where I'm about to take off there's a long stretch of road. So I've arrived at the spot where I've carefully planned and calculated it. I've parked my ute on the side of the road, I am now almost ready to action the plan, I've lit up a cigarette and going through the plan very carefully in my head, well this is what's going to happen, I will take off my seat belt start driving the ute up to one hundred and twenty kilometres an hour, and when I get close to the oncoming heavy truck I will collide with it head on and it will be all over, okay I'm thinking about this, today I'm doing this, I've been here parked for about two and a half hours, had quite a few more cigarettes thought a lot about it and yes finally I'm ready, let's do this I thought, here I go started the ute put it in gear my foot pressing the clutch I realized my left leg trembling uncontrollably with a knee jerk reaction I let go of the clutch, in doing this the engine stopped, by this time it felt as if every single hair on my body was standing, I could feel my body stiffening to a point where it was becoming painful by the second, the ute didn't move much so I've leaned back in to my seat frozen I don't know for how long.

Slowly as I'm getting some normality back into my thoughts I realized one thing I didn't plan for, obviously lit up another cigarette went back to thinking that what if it didn't work and I live after the accident in a state where I might need care twenty four seven. I thought it would be totally unfair for the one I love ends up with the responsibility of caring for me for the rest of my useless life. I broke down and started to cry like a little boy, stayed in this spot for quite some time, after a quite a few more cigarettes, and mixed feelings that I didn't go through with it, sad and at the same time glad that it didn't happen, now seventeen months later where I've communicated with people who've tried and I've communicated with people who have lost loved ones.

With this experience I've realized that I did not survive suicide. I wasn't ready for it, I did not have enough strength to do it today but for some strange reason I will feel the pilot light will always be burning and will never go out. I didn't write all this to glorify the situation, I guess I revealed this weakest and the darkest point of my life to let people who are suffering with similar intentions that we're not alone.

Anyway I hope I don't have to talk about this again or relive it. however I have learned a lot from this experience one of them is that we're not all the same, we don't all have the same ability to deal with our demons, a lot of us do come out of this ordeal, some of us use the strength to walk down the path of suicide thinking it's the walk of shame or the walk of triumph. It's very hard to put on the scale of what is worth and what isn't worth to live. At the end of the day it is entirely up to each individuals conception of which path one would walk on, so the bottom line is that no matter what anyone says or what anyone tries to do, the decision is already made on which path the troubled person will walk on. And besides all that when you've knocked on the pearly gates and got rejected and even the angel of death rejected your request of entering the pearly gates that's when you realize there's something different about the future that you're going to be leading, life feels totally different, you totally loose good friends and some valuable family members, well

I guess you can be fair on some people but for some people you've been there for them through some very dark times they've gone through no matter day or night no matter what time of the day or the night, you've dropped whatever was happening in your life to be there for them, and when you lifted your hand up for some of these so called good friends and some valued family members all you heard was they are too busy or they just don't have the time for you right now, well maybe I shouldn't be too hard on these people, maybe they don't have any knowledge or any experience on how to deal with suicidal people.

Well maybe after reading all this they might understand that people who have suicidal ideations already feel useless and worthless, by being ignored and avoided by people who they've trusted can only be a confirmation of being useless and worthless, it's a very sad situation that we only realize how important someone is to us after they are gone, without going any further about this what all this does is that it makes you become very selective on the subject of who you can trust and who you can rely on when the chips are down. Well around about this time of my life I can honestly say without any hesitations is that my dear wife and my loyal son were the only ones that are helping me through these very dark times of my life.

April 20, 21, and 22, 2019.
Three days of constant blur, uncertainty not knowing what to think, how to act or how to react, what to do and what not to do, I'm at a total loss here, can't talk to anyone can't see anyone, it feels as if I'm ashamed of being where I am without any control at all, I actually feel suffocated and where I am at the moment feels too deep and too dark too powerful, no way out. The time goes ever so slowly every minute feels like an hour, every hour feels like a day, and all the useless stuff that goes around and around in my head is like an absolute whirlpool that sucks me in deeper and deeper. So life goes on no matter what's in your head or what's happening in your day that feels like a useless life on daily basis. Again more breathing difficulties and lots more tears, hard to control .

April 23, 2019.
Been to see the OHS manager and distribution manager at my employment today to receive a two page return to work program for me to be on light duties. I've emailed it both to my lawyers and the union, so I'm going back to work tomorrow. We'll see what happens when I get there tomorrow, but the rest of the day is as usual, being miserable and not being able to see anything in the horizon at all. Thank god that I don't consume any alcohol at the moment, only plenty of coffee and lots of cigarettes that seems to help me through the day and night with a very limited hours of sleep with a combination of physical and mental pain that don't seem to ease at all, it is constant and it is extremely difficult to explain this to anyone, well it might be sad that people don't make time to come and see you let alone listen to you, so for some strange way even if you are in a crowded place you feel alone and without understanding you find yourself feeling lonely, so once again I find myself wandering and crying in the backyard and in the dark corner of my house, and yes at times it gets confusing that I don't want to go to bed at night because it's the same drama with the pain on my shoulder and my forearm so I don't get enough sleep and yet I don't want to get out of bed in the morning because I'm tired and did not get enough sleep and I will face another day with lots of uncertainties, so I go through another day no matter what happens or how I feel. Again that's life, whether you like it or not you get to learn to except, it is what is and you are on your own.

April 24, 2019.
Today I went back to work with a sling on my left arm from 6.00 am till 2.30 pm, it was quite obvious that I couldn't do anything physically, my task for the day was to go in to the loading bay and make sure that loads on trucks were done properly and safely, but what was disturbing is that if I did not checked the trucks it felt that it really did not matter, so it brings me back to the point that was I really being targeted on twenty second of March twenty nineteen, yeah it was light duties business as usual, no concern of my well being at all, actually it was quite disturbing and downgrading for

me walking around with my left arm in a sling, THAT'S LIFE I thought, and when I left my work place for the day I felt that I was made to feel worthless and useless knowing that for the last eleven years I thought I was invincible I thought I was unbeatable I thought nothing would get me down, wow how wrong was I while I'm travelling home in tears crying like a little boy but until the day of the surgery on my left shoulder I just wanted to put my head down and face whatever the challenges and whenever I was to be presented with anything, I needed to be ready but in saying that I now know it's easier said than done, well we're always faced with new challenges in life so this is a new one for me and I'm always trying to be optimistic about tomorrow being a new day and hopefully a better day. So once I get home it's the usual misery and hopelessness and still absolutely nothing on the horizon, back to the unlimited coffees and cigarettes, it truly feels like this is the way of living from here on, how sad.

April 25, 2019.
Anzac day public holiday today so I don't have to go in to my work place today to face the same agonizing and miserable day again, so early in the morning I decided to go and visit my mum, that's the only place I feel absolutely comfortable, I don't get judged or interrogated by my mum, it truly feels sacred, my mum's place to me at the moment is like a house of worship, in saying all that about my mum's place though my own house is a bit different, I just don't want to see my wife looking sad and uncertain about what's happening to me at the moment, me personally I'm finding whatever is happening to me now extremely hard to understand and most importantly very hard to except, but the mindset I'm trying to have is that life goes on and it must.

April 26, 2019.
I have an appointment today at 4.30 pm ultra sound on my forearm, first and last acknowledgement for my forearm until much later date I'll write about all that when we get to November 2019. I also have an appointment with physio today at 12.00 pm, these

two appointments today was instigated by the insurer, the thing I couldn't understand about the physio today is that why would I need the physio treatment on an injured shoulder?

But I strongly felt the need to follow every instruction that was thrown in my way by the insurer and every professional treader that I'm yet to see and face the music, anyhow with the ultra sound today was a bit weird the person that attended to do the ultra sound on my forearm was on the mobile phone the whole time, I guess that went okay I'll wait for the results to go to my treating doctor, not sure how long that will take, and then the physio well! Had some cream rubbed on sore areas on and around the shoulder and then I had some bandages put on the shoulder area and I was advised to put ice pack on the sore areas, well this advice actually felt like asking me to put a bandaid on lacerated areas on my body, but I feel that I need to go along with it as best as I can, just need to do my best, after all I truly want my shoulder and forearm injury to be repaired. And I was at work today, just as usual depressing and downgrading, I've only checked one truck today, I wasn't asked to do so I just wanted to help my team member simply because the load on the truck he loaded was not restrained properly so I did not want him to get in trouble.

The point to all this is that every single truck that was loaded by our forklift operators was meant to be checked before any of the trucks leaving the designated loading bays and obviously this was getting me more and more angry and upset and once again making me feel that I was targeted on the twenty-second of March twenty nineteen one week after my injury claim was excepted, I just couldn't figure out why this was happening.

April 27, 2019.

Not much sleep again last night, the pain on my shoulder the pain on my forearm and most importantly the pain in my head, constantly thinking of a lot of things that are both necessary and unnecessary things that are going around and around in my head, not seeing any light at the end of my tunnel, the suicidal ideation is like a pilot light, it almost feels like it's ready to ignite at any moment but these are the feelings I cannot talk to anyone, besides even if I wanted to talk to anyone it felt as if no one had the time for me I found that everyone was too busy dealing with their own misery or simply just having fun, I felt as if I wasn't important enough for anybody except my loyal wife and my loyal son.

I simply did not want them to know what was happening in my life right now, anyhow after a lousy night got out of bed this morning about 3.30 am made myself a coffee grabbed my ever so faithful cigarettes and as usual went outside into the darkness, I found that I'm trying my hardest not to think negatively but it's not working at all, I keep coming back to the same things in my head, by this time it's about 6.30 am I've already had four coffees and countless cigarettes my dear wife joins me with another fresh coffee and sits with me till about 8.30 am, conversations between my wife and I now are not the same.

I'm trying my best not to show her my anger I'm trying not to show her that I'm down and just about out so without wanting our conversations became very limited and very selective, not by choice that's just the way it is now a days, but the highlight of my day today is that my son came to see me. It was great to see him and have a cup of coffee with him, so from about 12.30 pm onwards not much else was happening, watched a bit of TV and trying to control the pain on my shoulder and my forearm with useless pain killers and antidepressants again, not very productive and certainly no fun at all, life still goes on, just.

April 27, 2019.
Up and out of bed at 2.35 this morning in pain and my head full of negative thoughts and obviously negative ideas just can't seem to be able to help myself, no control at all, again started my early morning with coffees and cigarettes until the sun came up, the rest of the day consuming more pain killers then I should and feeling worthless and useless again and the antidepressants are only numbing my scull temporarily until I take the next pill the next day and that's how the cycle continues to keep me feeling like a zombie.

One day I will be well enough and brave enough to elaborate on this issue that the antidepressants are useless and they don't work.

April 28, 2019.
Up at 2.30 this morning just couldn't go back to bed, just another quite and useless day not much happening, except I've heard from one of my long-time friend and his wife today, I have known them for forty-five years, we had a great chat, they showed a great deal of concern for my situation, I found out that they are in a similar situation as I am so it really was great to have them hear me and they actually listened to what I was saying, a hell of a lot more than anyone else and certainly lot more than any of my medical treaders, anyway in saying that they are not trained professionals so at the end of the day I go back to square one again.

Another thing I'm finding about all this is how slow the time is going, every minute feels like an hour, the days and nights are so painful so dark and so lonely, I truly wish that I had some hope and some reasonable amount of optimism that I can believe everything will be alright, but even if there was any hope or optimism I guess at the moment it is too dark for me to see or feel anything, sad but true just can't help feeling this way. SUCH IS LIFE.

Chapter 5

April 29, 2019.
Up and out of bed very early this morning with an unbearable pain running from my left shoulder all the way down to my wrist, shaking my head side to side, some more pain killers coffee and offcourse my loyal cigarettes and out into the back yard in the dark, what I'm starting to call this is my wilderness, anyhow had an appointment with work injury doctor this morning at 11.00 am, had a fruitless conversation about my mental stability and a little bit about the pain on my shoulder and my forearm I was offered more pain killers and antidepressants. Again not much else for the rest of the day and night.

April 30, 2019.
Six o'clock start work this morning, I mentioned to my manager at 6.30 about the loads on trucks not being checked and by 8.30 am all of us in distribution got together and had a tool box meeting about loads on trucks being checked and the procedure of checking trucks was back in place once again not knowing for how long, okay back to work again with me on light duties making sure that every load on every truck was restrained properly and left the loading bays safely.

So about 9.30 am I was called to go and see my manager, and the request from my manager was if I could get on the motorized industrial sweeper to go around and sweep the whole yard clean, I had to explain to my manager that if could drive the sweeper I might as well get on my fork lift and perform my daily tasks of loading and unloading trucks which I definitely can't at the moment, with my physical inability and mental instability at the moment I truly don't know why my manager would ask me to perform such a task, yeah some questions went through my mind, was total disrespect or was it to find out if I'm faking it all, unless my manager and company I'm working for are open and honest with me I'll never know, but I'm leaning more and more towards the idea that there is a total lack of respect and definitely no care factor at all, This is where I get the feeling of confirmation of being useless and worthless, half of the time I'm starting to understand that peoples lack of understanding and total ignorance and down grading attitude can push someone like me over the edge, well these are the times when I sit and do a lot of thinking this comes to my head, No one gives a rats so what's the POINT and it goes on and on.

May 1, 2019.

Back to work again today on light duties, waiting to get a date for surgery on my left shoulder, half of the time I'm thinking that I shouldn't be at work, I know one thing for sure that it is aggravating the pain on both my shoulder and my forearm, and the way I'm being treated at work it really is elevating my anger and anxiety levels right up and this is something I can't show or tell anyone, I am starting to understand and except that no one really cares about how I really feel or what I'm going through, anyhow I was called to go and see my manager this morning at 9.00 am.

    He told me that at any given time of the day I can go to any of the forklift operators and ask them to stop what they are doing and ask them to clean the yard, when I tried to explain to him that we don't have extra team member in the yard and that every team member had set tasks to prepare customer orders, load and unload trucks so there for it wouldn't be a clever task for me to perform as a team leader, after hearing this from me my manager informed me that if he had to do my job there was no reason and no point for me to be here in my work place, this is not something I wanted to hear from my manager, I thought we were more than just colleagues I thought we were friends before my work injury claim, anyway once again I went home with skin full of shit, and starting to have less respect towards my work place and my colleagues. Rest of the afternoon and night usual darkness. Life goes on and it must!!

May 2, 2019.
Back to work again on light duties, had a quite day did what I had to do, until towards the end of my shift, again I was called in to my managers office for something totally stupid and useless, it was about the yard and how to push and get more out of the forklift operators, the way he spoke to me was intimidating and I felt bullied so there for I stood up and stormed out of his office kicking and punching his door, I did not swear at him, I just told him that it was bullshit and I shouldn't be treated like this and went to the lunchroom to have a coffee and a cigarette to calm myself down.

And then left for the day to go home and stew in the same misery again for the afternoon and the night, with each of these conversations I have with people like my manager each time is escalating the percentage of my uselessness and worthiness, unfortunately not many people realises how heavy and how real this is.

May 3, 2019.
Back to work again, I just want to have less negative attitude and thoughts today so early this morning I called my manager to meet me near the lunchroom to have a coffee with me, and he did I apologized for my outburst yesterday and that I just wanted to get on with my day and do my job to the best of my ability, the conversation with him was okay.

However I went and seen the OHS manager to inform him of what happened and how it ended, and that I did not want any trouble, so there for I don't know if there was any discussion at all between my manager and the OHS manager, I guess I'll never know. And again for the rest of the day it was the same usual thing that none of the loads on any of the trucks was made compulsory to be checked at all, strange but true, so it's quite obvious that this kind of abnormality puts some heavy negativity in my head that I come home with skin full of shit, anyway on the way home seen the physio again at three pm and that was another negative treatment for the physio to work on my injured shoulder and my forearm . the rest of the afternoon and night very quiet and in pain where it leaves me with no other option but to take more pain killers, that's life I guess I just need to do my best until the surgery day, whenever that is.

May 4, 2019.

Today I'm organizing some appointments and sending some documents to the insurer, because of the increased pain on my left shoulder and my left forearm my treating doctor put my left arm in a sling so therefore I'm unable to drive my ute so the insurer has been issuing me with taxi vouchers.

Made an appointment to see my family doctor to get copies of the time I had off when this all started, in total about fifteen days, that was late March and early April this year, in the hope that I'll get those fifteen absent days reinstated back in to my account, so the rest of the day and night again very quite with unlimited coffees and cigarettes and trying to slip out this miserable feelings and thoughts, thoughts like distancing myself from everybody, I feel that I'm not in the mood to talk to anyone and I certainly am not in the mood to listen to anyone else's issues, in doing that I do realize that I am losing some family members and good friends that I thought would have been there for me but that's another sad issue that I have to deal with, as I mentioned before the ones that I thought I could count on and depend on are all too busy and absolutely no effort or time is being made for me at all, that's life.

May 5, 2019.

Up and early again this morning, the beginning of a usual sad, unsettled and depressed day, yeah feeling sad especially for my wife, she's never seen me like this before I see the sadness in her eyes that she seems to find it extremely hard to hide, that hurts and upsets me even more than I already feel, even though I try my hardest to put a smile on my face because we've been together for so long she can see right through me.

I do end up going outside with my coffee and cigarettes deep in to the corner of the backyard somewhere where I can stew in my own misery again until bed time, yes somehow I do understand that's not the way to live but I just can't help myself, yeah another day gone sad, angry, sorry and feeling all alone with my useless thoughts.

Chapter 6

May 6, 2019.
Sent an envelope to my lawyer today explaining what's been happening so she can be kept up to date with my daily activities, had another session with psychologist today and she told me that the insurer needs to be informed about my mental health situation, I will discuss it with both my family doctor and the insurance doctor in the next few days.

Oh by the way I mentioned to my psychologist that a couple of weeks ago I was suicidal and that I almost ended it all, and her response was for me not to be stupid and not to do anything silly, wow I thought that was the last thing I would want to hear from a professional telling me not to be stupid and the best thing she could do was to give me two phone numbers for me to get help, me being angry and not in the right state of mind I asked her directly how the hell can anybody help me when I'm about to pull the trigger, is that the right time for me to use one of these phone numbers and ask them what? Do I ask the person on the other end of the phone on how to pull the trigger? What happens afterwards? Or when is it the right time?

Now I'm finding myself getting more and more angry, but I feel I need to keep on seeing this psychologist because of the strong recommendations of both my family doctor and my injury treating doctor. Well coming home with all this shit in my head was not pleasant at all, I thought it was totally unacceptable being told not to be stupid by a professional psychologist, the rest of the day and night just the usual, quite and alone in my own thoughts, Even if I wanted to bother anyone apart from my wife and my son there's no one else there that can really understand the conversation I've had today with the psychologist. At this point if I wasn't deep enough in my dark thoughts days like today can really push a person even deeper in an uncertain and an unfamiliar place where a person has never been before, and with days like today getting home again with skin full of shit and what happens throughout the day it certainly doesn't make it any easier seeing the night through at all, not to mention the pain on left shoulder and left forearm aching constantly with or without painkillers.

Oh by the way I found out today that one of the afternoon shift worker dropped a bundle of twelve metre pipe onto a truck in the loading bay that could have been fatal because there's always someone near the parked trucks opening the gates on the trucks or tying down the loads on the trucks, now this accident happened with a forklift where it is forbidden to perform this task, there's a designated side loader to perform this loading procedure where it was totally ignored, now the sad and disturbing part of all this is there was no counselling or any written warnings given to the forklift operator, so again knowing this really heightens my stress levels to the max, the question in my head again, was I deliberately and cunningly targeted? Hopefully one day it will all be revealed.

May 7, 2019.

Seen the surgeon today at 1.30 pm at Epworth private hospital in Richmond about rotator cuff repair on my left shoulder, at the end of the consultation it was confirmed that the surgery will take place at Epworth private hospital at hawthorn on the twelfth of June at one pm, this was the only positive thing today, something for me to look forward to that finally after six years of hiding my pain and diligently working right through at last something was positively getting done, oh by the way the insurer is supplying me with taxi's to and from all my medical treaders, however when I get home the usual anger, the anguish, the uselessness and the worthlessness inevitably continues all hours of the night and in most cases in to the day light.

I never ever thought that I would ever go through any of these emotions at all but that's life, I'm hoping that one day I will have the opportunity to tell my story to someone that might actually care and listen to what I have to say, yeah I'm optimistic and very hopeful, we all get told never to give up hope but as we all know talking is cheap so there you go.

May 8 and 9, 2019.
These two days I've had a lot of emptiness, nothing in the horizon and most discouragingly there's definitely no light at the end of the tunnel, once again I definitely don't want to associate with anyone, I feel I have no interest in any useless conversations with anyone at all, it's one of those day's again I just want to be left alone and stew in my own misery with extreme difficulty to hide it from my wife and my son, I guess I really appreciate and respect their love and unconditional loyalty towards me I truly don't want them to see me in this state at all, after all I have been the tower of strength to my wife and my children all these years and I would like to continue to be a good husband and a good dad.

May 10, 2019.
Had an appointment with my family doctor this morning at 9.30 am for a general check up on my health and wellbeing, for the reasons that I do have excessive amounts of coffees and cigarettes, and at 11.00 am had another appointment with work injury doctor, the usual doctor wasn't in today so the supplement doctor I had was not accommodating and he had a lack of interest in how he was handling my case so I angrily walked out of consulting room, one good thing is that I didn't lose it terribly and I did not swear at anyone.

I think that with all the pain killers I've been taking and my left arm being in a sling and not being able to drive is not helping my moods at all, so there for I cannot wait to get home quick enough to get in to the back yard of the house with my coffee an my cigarettes find somewhere to sit and call it a safe haven where no one else disturbs me.

May 11 and 12, 2019.
I did not feel like writing about anything these two days, I just felt lost, these two days at home late at night had some uncontrollable trembling moments, bit of a rage that it was a good thing I was at home. I don't want to elaborate on this any further I did go through some painful blank moments. We'll see what happens tomorrow.

May 13, 2019.
Back to work today, maybe I shouldn't mention this but again there are no requests being made to check any of the loads on any of the trucks, so of course this keeps the feeling of me being targeted on the twenty second of March this year well alive in my head that causes the stress and anxiety levels to rise, not to mention the anger.

Anyhow mid to late morning I had a chance to have a long discussion with the OHS manager about a few important issues, one of them was how I almost ended it all a few weeks ago which he was not aware of, our conversation was quite intense and got very emotional that a close member of his family had committed suicide recently so that our conversation was taken very seriously, in a way I guess it was good because not long after the conversation with the OHS manager I received a phone call from the insurers case manager that the date for my shoulder surgery was approved for the sixteenth of June, how ironic I've been waiting for this confirmation for a while now, and again quite ironically I've received another phone call, this time it was from my physiologist, telling that if I needed an urgent session to give her call and another phone call from the physiologist again at six pm checking up on me to see if I'm okay, all this happened today because of the OHS manager was a bit concerned and made a couple of phone calls.

Well it's just a waiting game now with a sore shoulder, sore forearm and a messed up head, it seems impossible to build up any confidence in any area of my life at the moment that everything is going to be alright, I just can't see any light at the end of the tunnel, again life goes on and it must.

May 14, 2019.

Back to work again today with no heart, no soul, no passion, no respect, no loyalty and no diligence, practically dragging my feet, it is incredibly unbelievable how people can change, people in charge can make you feel so worthless and so useless, hey life goes on if you let it, still not in a good space, I don't want to see anyone, I don't want to talk to anyone I just want to be left alone, alone for good sometimes and right now I don't even want to think about anything at all, hopefully tomorrow will be a better day, six twenty eight pm today I received a phone call from the psychologist asking me if I wanted a session soon and again at six forty from the psychologist's office trying to get me an appointment as soon as possible and we've locked one in for this Monday coming where we sit down and have more fruitless conversations.

Well for the rest of the day it's just the usual misery and dark thoughts, I find myself walking out in the back yard with a coffee and a cigarette thinking I'll sit in the corner of the yard for about ten minutes, however three to four hours later coming back to some kind of reality only to realize that I've been crying again wiping my tears off of my cheeks, another dark, alone and miserable night going to bed with aching head, shoulder and forearm, this is starting to feel like a new way of life where I feel the need to adjust to it, simply because at the moment I just don't know how to change anything in my life, lots of down time and lots of darkness still, nothing on the horizon.

May 15, 2019.

Not much to write about today, the misery and the aches and pains are continuing so dramatically from yesterday and last night that I'm finding it extremely hard to shake it off, so it was a total isolation all day and all night, did not feel like associating with anyone today, I guess I was trying to make some sense out of all this going on in my head, no solution and it feels like there's no way out except the unimaginable and the unacceptable, as much as I don't want to go there, I don't want to contemplate the ideation of ending it all, the feeling is still very fresh as I mentioned before the pilot light never goes out, it's with me all day every day, hopefully someday, somewhere, someone will sit with me hear me out and maybe just maybe will have the ability to understand me for exactly what it is.

May 16, 2019.
Another fruitless day at work today, again it was so degrading the morale is not there, it truly feels like there's an invisible line between my team members and I, the bond is broken, that happens to be with every person I had worked with all these years wow!! That's unbelievable and truly unacceptable but hey there's nothing I can do about it, and the managers again wow!

They would not give me the time of the day, how sad, the managers I'm talking about are the ones that used to reward me with vouchers and bottles of whiskey for doing such a great job, yeah it does make me wonder why the change of attitude and personality and most importantly the mutual respect we all had for one and other, anyhow as I'm checking a load on one of the trucks today I've noticed the load was unsafe so therefore I've called the forklift operator that was responsible for this load and as I'm trying to explain the issue to him to my total shock I was told to f#@* off twice and this was coming from one of my team members that I thought we had mutual respect for each other, wow! I think momentarily I just froze this was totally unexpected, I just did not know what to say or what to do so I just walked away in total disbelieve so yes this incident made my head worse than it already was.

Now I'm thinking when you are made to go to work on light duties knowing you are not ready can have a lot worse affect on anybody's recovery process, I now strongly believe that most employers and work injury insurers don't understand and if they do they simply don't care no care factor at all, it really is very disappointing, by now you probably wandering why am I putting up with all this unnecessary disappointment? Well I cannot afford to stop working until the surgery date, my ongoing bills are not allowing me to do so, so yes this does put me in a very vulnerable position on top of the personal mental and physical issues I'm already dealing with so yes! It really does get harder and harder to deal with all this on daily basis, so again these are the times where I seriously start questioning myself is this all worth it? How long? And why? It really does get scary.

When all these thoughts are going around and around in my head I somehow feel like a leaf in a ferocious storm, I don't know what's ahead but at the moment none of this feels normal and it doesn't feel good at all, and I'm still shocked on how disappointing it is that I've lost friends whom I thought were trustworthy and dependable and some family members on the same category wow! I found it absolutely pathetic when these low quality people telling me how busy they are and more or less telling me that they have no time for me no matter how desperate I've become at times. Anyway the rest of the night as usual more coffees and more cigarettes and whenever I end up going to bed inevitably more pain killers, wether I like it or not this seems like my new regular life style now, no other option now.

May 17, 2019.
Up and out of bed early today trying to elevate my confidence and strength to get through the day at work, when I arrived at work it was just as I anticipated, no trucks were looked at and no loads on any of the trucks were getting checked, only if and when I'm near the loading bays at my leisure I'm trying to make a concerted effort to check the loads for safety purposes, I'm still finding it strange that no request has been made by any of the forklift operators to check any of the loads, just another uncertain day at my work place today, there's definitely no respect and the bond is gone, I really feel so alone, and of course all this makes me think that when you're injured at work and you can no longer perform your usual tasks it almost feels like the people you've worked with for so long have a united way of making you feel useless and worthless, they making me think that they don't believe me at all they must think that I'm faking my pain and my mental state, just can't help thinking this way.

The pain on my left shoulder and my forearm and my mental state and the treatment I get from my teammates by the time I get home I feel so drained that towards the middle of the evening I find myself in the quite part of the back yard at home licking my wounds and trying so hard to stay strong, this is not easy at all, looking at the clock and seeing one minute pass feels like a whole hour, I keep doing this until I go to bed and at times it could be two or three o'clock in the morning before I actually make it to bed.

May 18 and 19, 2019.
Two whole days and nights of darkness and feeling down, not much to say and really don't want to associate with anyone, I've lost something very valuable in my head and in my heart, it's the care factor, I don't seem to have the ability to care for anything or anyone at the moment, yeah it's sad but I just can't help it, I just don't know what to do or where to go with this.

May 20, 2019.
Seen the psychologist today, I felt that she was struggling with me today, I felt as if she sensed my anger and my frustration even though she comes across that she's old enough and experience enough but I felt that she was trying a bit too hard to deal with me and my issues, I felt that talking to her and listening to her today was absolutely fruitless and totally useless and a total waste of time, it felt like she had no idea and asking some totally irrelevant questions and obviously this had made me more angry and more frustrated that I couldn't wait to get out of there.

When I finally got home the rest of the day and night was the same old uselessness, uncertainty and very dark moments until I finally went to bed. Again that's life for now.

Chapter 7

May 22, 2019.
I've seen the work injury doctor today, after speaking with her about what's been happening and how I've been coping with my anger and frustration she referred me to see a psychiatrist, here I go I thought, this is getting bad this is getting serious, on the way home in the back seat of a taxi there's this sadness and hurtful feelings starting set itself deep in my thoughts, this made me become a bit tearful I actually started to cry like little boy in the taxi, I was actually thinking that I've lost my mind and the referral to see a psychiatrist was the confirmation of that which I found it totally unacceptable thinking that I'm already seeing a psychologist and why do I need to see a psychiatrist as well?

I've never thought I'll come to this point in my life, I always thought of myself as being a well balanced and well adjusted person for a long time. So it really wasn't easy going home with this new and unwanted referral at all, but I feel I need to follow the recommendations of any of the medical treaders, so when I get a chance I need to find a psychiatrist and make the first appointment. Anyhow when I arrived home it was the same old usual evening and night, still no light at the end of the tunnel. Just struggling in the dark.

May 23, 2019.
Not much different today, I've seen my family doctor for some stronger pain killers, the rest of the day and night was same old messed up head and the usual pain on shoulder and forearm. That's it.

May 24, 25 and 26, 2019.
Three days and nights nothing to say and nothing to write about, it was all blank, blank and blank, I guess I'm just getting too sick and tired of writing about the same misery about my head and my aches and pains, just totally and totally sick of it all. That's all for now I don't want to think, talk or write anything else today.

May 27, 2019.
Seen the psychologist this morning, had a chat with her about my mental stability and that I find myself in a rage at times that it worries me, and to my shock she gave me two phone numbers for organisations that can maybe can help people like me, wow!

I thought this is the best this professional can do for me, Actually this made me more angry and more annoyed that it's the best these professionals can do, they have the ability to hand ball you from one organisation to another, by now I'm thinking that even if you are in a normal state of mind all this f@#^ing bull@#$^ is enough to push anyone over the edge, I really mean when I say no one cares or gives a rats arse, yes I am angry almost in a rage now, I now except that no one has any idea or full understanding, professionalism or any knowledge at all to help people with mental health issues, all the knowledge they think they have is all based on assumptions.

The only way people take you seriously no matter who they are, professionals, family members or friends is if and when you actioned the unexpected by ending it all at once, that's when people take notice of you, in most cases it's too late. Anyway I have found a psychiatrist, they need an approval from the insurer so I can't make an appointment until I get the approval, so I have to wait patiently, too bad if I was about to make the very last decision of my life, oh well it's only me, not important enough, I except that for some reason it makes me deal with it all a bit easier that there are no high expectations so just wait.

May 29, 2019.
Made an appearance at work again today with my left arm in a sling, I feel the need to wear the sling because with constant ache on left

shoulder and left forearm and when I walk constant swinging of my left arm escalates the pain so it almost feels like I have no option but to wear the sling, anyway at work today again no request has been made to check any of the loads on any of the trucks, only if I'm available or if I make the effort to go in to the loading bays to check loads for safety, so again this does enrages the thoughts in my head as to why I've received the first and final warning for one of the trucks I've loaded was not safe, so they've told me, but now every truck is leaving the loading bays without being checked.

So for now this is something I have to except even though it may be unfair, unacceptable and unlawful at the moment I just don't have the mental capacity to deal with it. Since all this started on the twenty-ninth of March I have used some of my sick leave and roster day entitlements so when I've seen the work injury Doctor today I mention this so I have to wait and see if I will receive any of it back.

June 3, 2019.
I haven't written anything last few days, it's all the same routine, spending a lot of my time on my own, I know I'm stewing in my own misery but I'm not hurting anyone, constantly want to be left alone, yes it does get dangerous at times especially with self harm ideations that never seems to go away from my thoughts, but I do my best to keep the lid on it, and one of the reasons why I choose not to talk to anybody about my issues is that I hear from people that similar thing has happened to one of their uncles or one of their cousins.

I'm just not interested at all, I know that we all have our own issues and we all have a different ways of handling our own issues none of us are the same, I strongly feel that spending alone time in my own space is a lot safer for me, sometimes when I am being compared to someone's distant relative can really rise the levels of anger to the point of explosion where I don't want to hurt people either physically or verbally, yeah it does get really hard to keep the lid on at times, but I'm trying to do my best.

June 5, 2019.

Again back at work as usual, the level of communicational skills and the level of respect from my team members and the officials are very low, now what people don't understand is that this puts some very dangerous thoughts in my head, maybe I am a bad person maybe I am not worthy of their attention and maybe I am totally useless maybe I should call it quits maybe I shouldn't be here on this earth at all, being ignored can make a person to take the path where you only get to make one last decision, yeah call it quits well I'm not there yet, anyway I am at work today as well as any other day for bureaucratic reasons, very unpleasant, as long as I've clocked on and I'm here it doesn't seem to matter what I do all day, to be honest I'm doing jack shit all day, walking around pretending that I'm checking some product other times sitting in despatch office looking for things to do and occasionally.

I go out into the loading bays to check on some loads on trucks, still there are no requests been made by anyone to check any of the loads on any trucks, thinking that I received my first and final warning because the truck I've loaded on March twenty second according to my officials was not safe, but now none of the trucks are getting checked, never mind I'll just go along with it.

June 5, 2019.

Seen the work injury doctor today, one of our topic today was to get my sick leave entitlements back that I've lost late March to mid April, I don't like my chances but I'll give it a go, see what happens good luck, anyhow at my lunch break today I've noticed a semi trailer in the exit driveway bound for Mildura.

I had a feeling that it wasn't checked in the loading bay, so I went over to check and sure enough couple of the bundles of large coils were not restrained safely on the trailer, after explaining the safety procedures and company's policies to the driver he done the right thing and secured the load safely, now this left me scratching my head thinking what do I do, do I report this to the officials that had given me my first and final warning and get one of my disrespectful team members in trouble at the risk of him getting a first and final warning as well ? I do have a footage of this on my mobile. It was exactly the same case when I received my warning. Severe breech of f%$#@ safety, so there you go.

NO I did not report it, at the end of the day when I got home again it was as usual with the afternoon and the night, usual pain on left shoulder and left forearm, taking pain killers and mentally slipping into deep and dark thoughts again and again, not knowing what's ahead, not knowing what to do, no hope no confidence, feeling powerless and useless, smoking and drinking countless cups of coffee until the early hours of the morning, waiting for the sun to come up to begin another useless day again, this happens a lot. But at the moment I seem to have no other options except to be patient, hoping that one day this will all go away and I will be back to my normal self again.

Yeah this gives me a very low level of optimism that creates a small percentage of comfort that disappears within minutes.

June 11, 2019.

I haven't written anything the last few days again, it's all the same thoughts the same feelings, yes it does become annoying constantly stewing in the same misery day in day out, so at times I do become reluctant to write about anything, however there's one good thing to look forward to is that tomorrow is the day of the surgery on my left shoulder, for some reason this does lift the level of optimism a little higher thinking that after the surgery and with some good and consisting rehab things might get back to normal, yeah well one would always hope I guess.

Chapter 8

June 12, 2019.
The day for the surgery is finally here, we'll see what happens from here onwards. Okay I have arrived at the private hospital in hawthorn at 12.30 pm appointment at 1.00 pm so I've checked in fill out some more forms and the waiting has began, not knowing what to expect and waiting ever so patiently and constantly checking my mobile phone that I made sure that it was charged to one hundred percent, yeah waiting for the well wishers to call me and comfort me in some way, wow how ironic the only two people called me were my wife and my son, well this leaves a very little space in my heart and in my thoughts for the people that whispers sweet nothings into my ear, telling me how close and good friends and family members we are, yeah right!!.

Anyhow I waited patiently until 5.50 pm and then taken into the operating room, woke up in the recovery room at about 7.20 pm obviously a bit groggy, my arm was covered in bandages with some hard plastic from my shoulder all the way down to my wrist, apparently the surgery was good and the nurses were great, they were checking up on me right throughout the night, I did manage to have dinner and I was able to get up and go to the toilet. Oh yeah there is a glimpse of hope that everything is going to be all right.

June 13, 2019.
Woke up this morning, again the nurses were absolutely fantastic, checking my blood pressure and giving me pain killers, early in the morning the surgeon came in and told me that the

surgery went very well even though the tear was bigger then what the scans showed, he assured me that everything was okay.

So I left the hospital with certain degree of satisfaction and peace, I arrived home about 10.00 am, even though I was looked after at the hospital it really was great to be home in my own environment, My dear wife could not do enough for me, god bless her heart and soul, around midday I become a bit cocky I took my arm of the sling as if nothing happened, late in the afternoon the pain started greater, even though I kept up with the pain killers, Okay starting to realise everything I do physically I must do it with utmost caution, need to except it is what it is, I am here now I feel it will be a long recovery, I must except and go with it.

June 14, 2019.

4.00 am out of bed, I'd like to say I just woke up but I did not sleep at all, not even one minute, I don't know what happened but between the shoulder and the forearm I was in a terrible pain all night, I could not find a comfortable position that I could rest and most importantly get some sleep, still keeping up with the pain killers and lack of sleep I'm starting to feel like a zombie now, my brother his wife and my mum came to visit this afternoon, trying to talk to them on the recliner I couldn't keep my eyes open, after they left I'm finding that I am in a lot pain, tired and sleepy, god only knows I'm trying to do my best for a speedy recovery both physically and mentally, speaking of mentally I know it's another issue and I also know that there are still a lot of hills and roads ahead.

I'm sure I'll do my very best to stay straight and narrow, I definitely don't want to play to lose I want to get over it and get on with my life for whatever it's worth.

June 15, 2019.

Got up early this morning, with about three hours of sleep last night it wasn't enough but it was better than nothing at all, I'm trying to have a good start to my day, shower, breakfast all good but the pain on the shoulder and the forearm only eases off between taking pain killers for a short period, not being in a right state of mind mentally is not helping at all, because I don't know how long the physical recovery period is so this allows me to sit here with my arm in a sling to go into the deep and dark corners of my mind over and over again, trying to find the reasons how the hell did I ended in this situation mentally, trying to find resolution, trying to hold someone responsible and accountable.

I don't know if all this is making me more and more angry to seek revenge, oh boy I'm starting to get scared just to think that I'm entertaining the idea of hurting someone or worse killing someone, wow this is not me but I'm struggling to find the answers why I'm feeling this way, by now cold sweat running down my forehead and my face that I'm in fear that I truly do want to find some sensible answers before it's too late, yeah I am worried, thankfully I am glad that I spend a lot of time on my own and in my own environment.

I know this is not healthy but I go through these thoughts just about every minute of the day, I really have no control of why I feel this way. No matter how optimistic I try to become I just can't lift the levels of my optimism high enough to have a good day, it just doesn't seem to work, it's really hard to except what I feel, how I feel and the things I want to do and the things I don't want to do, and then I come to the old saying that it is what it is. Just deal with it, no other option, REALLY?

June 16, 2019.
Not a very good night again, very little sleep and a lot of pain on the left shoulder and forearm for some reason, but I'm keeping it together for now it's a good thing I guess, I'm trying my best not to lose it, I am doing my absolute best not to run out of patience, so be it another day of full restrictions and isolations and my arm in a sling, oh boy this creates a very large opportunistic fields of dark feelings and very dark thoughts, the feelings the dark thoughts that I have never ever imagined before, I truly don't know if I am ever going to recover or be released from any of these feelings or thoughts.

I don't know how to explain this but there is a certain degree level of gladness within myself that I must have the ability to tap into my inner strength and use it wisely to keep me from going against all odds, I just hope that I don't run out of my inner strength, it obviously is helping me stay away from any regrettable actions and ideations for now.

Another down side to all this is that I spend a lot of time outside in the back yard just about every night with unlimited coffees and cigarettes, it almost feels like the coffees and the cigarettes are my only faithful friends and my only tools there are available for me to deal with it all, so it seems.

June 17, 2019.

Up and down all night again last night, very minimal sleep, spent a lot of time in and out of the lounge room, trying to watch TV I feel tired and sleepy decide to go to bed and then the excruciating pain on shoulder and forearm begins so back to the lounge room again this happens quite a lot, well nearly every night, it really does get very annoying, however I am trying very hard to control my pain, my mood swings and my stress levels especially in the presence of my wife day and night, this also gets very strenuous trying to have a fake a smile on my face, trying to give my wife a positive attitude where my mind is full of negative and dangerous thoughts not easy at all, but I am doing my absolute best to stew in my own misery privately and silently, as much as I don't give a rats arse about anyone else but for some reason with some powers from within allows me to consider my wife's emotions and happiness.

She don't deserve my misery and I truly don't want her to see me like this, it really isn't fair on her. Yeah lack of sleep and lots of deep thoughts does make me feel like a zombie the next day, quite often I feel as if I am stuck on a treadmill of self destruction just can't get off of it, apart from being physically unwell at the moment I just can't seem to control my state of mind, things like mentally how the hell did I get here at this point, why did I come to this point and more importantly thinking about the people who pushed me to this point, at the moment the way I'm feeling unfortunately I have no answers what so ever.

I might have an idea about who and why am I been pushed to this point, but I have no idea of what to do about it all, Maybe one day this will all be clear to me and everybody else. Here's a bit of a positive attitude "Life goes on "and IT MUST!!

June 18, 2019.
Hit the sack last night about eleven fifty and woken up by the pain at two thirty am straight to the kitchen grab a coffee and my cigarettes and found myself out in the backyard again, set myself up for a long haul, meaning that I'll be out here in the back yard god knows for how long, so here comes that thick dark cloud hanging so low above my head to the point of suffocation, breathlessness and in a state of panic, sure enough this does reignite bad and very negative thoughts in my head and here it is I'm crying like a little boy trying to except that none of this is my fault, I've cried for about twenty minutes not in silence in the dark corner of the back yard, momentarily it does feel good crying but it really doesn't solve any of my issues.

I could be surrounded by a thousand people but I still feel all alone, trying to talk to people but no one hears me and if any of the professionals hear me they only try and give me advice based on professional assumption, it feels as if the professionals are treating us mentally affected people as if we're all the same, to me it is clearly understood that we're all products and can be victims of our own choices, but I don't believe my situation was my choice, so this can clearly be misrepresentation when my issues are compared to someone else's or vice a versa, anyhow these are some of the things that goes through my mind constantly, and all this and more constantly puts me in a deeper and darker place and keeps me there for a long time, so many times I wish I could pick myself up and get back on the surface where I can breath and see a lot of things more clearly.

I'm still in the back yard I'll soon get up put a fake smile on my face and go in the house and try not to show the miserable side of me to my wife.

June 19, 2019.
Not much sleep again last night, in and out of bed at least six to eight times, at last around four am I went outside and stayed out until the sun came up, as usual more coffees and more cigarettes sometimes sitting around and sometimes walking around to find things to do with currently limited capacity I have both mentally and physically to deter my mind from going into dark unpleasant areas where it constantly keeps the pilot light alive.

It really isn't easy to keep the lid on at times, on top of all this with excessive use of pain killers I'm finding myself being constipated more often, that in itself is uncomfortable with mood swings and physical well being, at times like these I am very reluctant to go in the house where my wife is, it feels like I have to put on a happy mask for my wife and everyone else, and that gets me thinking that I have to hide behind the mask just to see the day through, not fair at all so this is where it all becomes like a whirlpool brings everything into one place in my mind and it takes me back to the start of all this, it also brings me back to the point of manifesting on how am I ever going to overcome this will it ever come to a pleasant end or will it turn out ugly, am I ever going to be free from all this resentment, am I going to end up with my life full of regrets.

I simply don't know for the moment, with all this going through my head constantly that it's becoming a new normal for me, I just can't explain it where I don't know and I don't understand it myself, optimism is so far away and hopefulness simply don't exist. At the moment words like don't give up, don't let go, hang in there are very cheap and they feel like they're all sweet whispers, none of them are valid and none of them have any value at all.

June 20, 2019.
Excessive pain killers and sleeping pills it wasn't too bad last night, less time spend out in the back yard and less crying, very quiet day today very flat both mentally and physically the anti depressants aren't working and if they are they are doing totally the opposite, the only thing the anti depressants are doing is that they are numbing my scull, making me feel weak, they actually making me

feel as if I'm walking around like a zombie, these anti depressants are actually keeping me down to the ground where my misery is, they are not helping at all and when I mention this to my medical professionals they all tell me to give it a chance yeah well I've been taken them for couple of months now with no improvement at all.

In my view about these anti depressants one of the scenario is that it is one of those carefully manifested and fabricated and very beneficial in the financial area for our medical professionals that they can prescribe these anti depressants to us in the hope that it will work and everything is going to be alright, I think I might find a large percentage of people who ever reads this would actually agree with me.

June 21, 2019.
I'm actually not in the mood or in a good space today to write about anything, no care factor today, much more flat than yesterday very quite day, don't want to talk, don't want to write, don't want to associate with anyone, I guess what I am trying to say is that I just want to be left alone, totally alone.

June 22 and 23, 2019.
Last couple of days are like 21st June no energy very flat don't know what to think about don't know what to write about zero interest in anything, all blank, continuing with pain management with pain killers including anti depressants, it almost feels like I've become a product of the system that wants me to remain stuck where I am.

This is where this all triggers the minds of people like me to take one of the three options, mental institution, jail or six foot under, it really isn't easy to live with these options unfortunately when you're down and just about out in the darkness these are the options you don't see but you feel the sadness and the hurtfulness is when you become hopelessly powerless and desperate to take one of these options, some of us do and some of us don't, so there for no one can make any judgement, have any opinion or make any assumptions on which option people take under these circumstances.

You see I didn't want to write about anything the last few days, because I don't write anything doesn't mean that my mind has a rest, no it just keep going and going twenty four seven, nonstop.

June 24, 2019.

Another one of those sleepless, uncomfortable and painful night both shoulder and forearm, had an appointment with the psychologist this morning at 9.15 I've cancelled it I simply don't feel up to it and not in the right state of mind at the moment, so I rescheduled my appointment the best they can do was the 19th of September, that's almost three months away WOW too bad if my situation was crucial and I desperately needed some professional help, oh but they were kind enough to tell me that if there was a cancellation between now and 19th of September they will let me know, yeah thanks for nothing I thought.

Had a long phone conversation with the case manager from the insurers office, I found out that she was not aware of my mental health issue and the severity of it, she demonstrated a lot of fruitless concern, only because she had to our conversation was being recorded so there for she had to show some professionalism to justify her existence in her work place, nothing gained nothing lost, however I did assure her that everything is okay I'm doing okay and she has nothing to be concerned about, except however the pilot light is always on.

It only goes to prove and confirm that I and everyone else who are in the same situation as I am are nothing but numbers, knowing this confirmation can also add more anger to every individual, anger? Because sometimes I do believe that our medical professionals can cause more harm than good to some of us mentally ill patients, simply ignoring and neglecting the real issues and concerns.

Giving me a bag full of anti depressants and sending me away should not be the only solution, however I guess just like everyone else I am learning to live with it. Then again the choice is simple, Stay or Leave!.

June 25, 2019.
Another unsatisfactory night, not enough sleep due to increasing pain on left forearm and shoulder, one of the main problems is that no matter what position I lay down in bed there seems to be no comfort, the effect of the pain killers only last around one hour, the excessive number of pain killers I take during the night makes me walk around like a zombie the next day, in turn this does affect my moods and yes it does make me more angry, can't help it.

Anyway I did receive a phone call today from the liaison lady we'll call her Miss X, she is from a consulting company that would do her absolute best in her power to get me back to work no matter what even if I'm bleeding she would want me to go back to work, She was appointed by the insurer so my case can end as soon as possible, anyhow she wants to attend to my first appointment with the surgeon the 2nd of July, I agreed to it without any hesitations at all, see what happens. At this very moment I'm finding myself wanting to write and reveal a lot things on these pages, but I don't think I should, I don't believe I'm ready yet and sometimes I don't know if I'll ever be ready or if I'm ever going to have the opportunity to be ready.

June 26 and 27, 2019.
Yesterday and today not in a good space, as usual these days feeling like a zombie, actually feeling like shit, I don't know what made me realize and remember this today it just dawned on me that I've lost my independence I can't see anything in the f*&^ing horizon yeah I'm swearing I'm angry, I feel hopeless and I feel useless, it's just another one of those days where I am stewing in my own misery, last thing I need right now is to socialize with anyone especially the fake and the useless people that were close to me before I hit the rock bottom.

I need to stop here and now before I spill anymore on these pages that I might regret for a very long time.

June 28, 2019.
Again limited sleep increased pain in the forearm again and again, stayed in my pyjamas all day, not much else to do except try and have more patience, try and see things more clearly, trying to find the real meaning of hope, trying to understand if I can live with hope or if I can live without hope, do I need to find religious or spiritual purposes to identify the reasons as to why am I living so hopelessly in a useless environment with so little capability in my day to day living both mentally and physically, yeah this brings me to the question is HOPE a myth?

Or Is it just a word that has been created by spiritual and religious leaders to keep us on straight and narrow path, one would also think of the word HOPE is an artificial amusement . I'm sure this can be debateable on so many different levels, maybe one day when I can fully get back to myself I can have this debate with whomever and when ever but not right now I truly have no mental capacity to continue to find if anything makes sense at all.

June 29, 2019.
I wish I could get out bed ever so enthusiastically today and say good morning to everyone, hug and kiss everyone, telling everyone how fantastic I feel and how my heart is filled with joy mmmmm that was just a moment where I came up to the surface took a deep breath and went back down again.

It was good to wish and it felt great even if it only lasted for one moment, not much else to hang on to, here I go getting angry again with the terrible feeling of what's been happening to me through hazy and blurry visions that I don't have the ability to make any sense out of it all, I'm getting sick of wearing this happy mask so none of this miserable stage I'm going through should upset my dear wife, she definitely doesn't deserve any of this, sometimes I just want to get away far away somewhere where there's no spiritual, religious or political gravity, just to float and glide through the air like a bird, again that's just another wish, well knowing it's another wish it certainly puts me back in to the area where I constantly keep on stewing in my own misery as usual, yeah looking at this from another angle is that I could end all this once and for all or stay strong and keep being patient and believing that one day this is all going to be alright.

I guess I do have a choice, anyway one of the main reasons of why I write all this on these pages are is that I don't talk to anyone, I simply don't associate with anyone there's no one out there that I can be open and honest about all this and I simply don't trust anyone, so that's how it goes.

July 1, 2019.
Another useless night, same as usual pain and pills, pain and pills how exciting, not much happening during the day with limited movement o left shoulder and forearm, watching a bit of TV and spending a lot of time writing about my daily activities, things like I don't want to be angry anymore, I don't want to be sad anymore, I don't want to be down or feel hurt anymore, I don't want to have any dangerous thoughts anymore but I just can't help it.

I just can't get over a lot of these issues overnight but hey I'm trying, consultation with the surgeon tomorrow first one since the surgery, yeah something to look forward to, get me out of the house for a few hours all the way to Richmond and back. Well rest of the day trying to find something positive on the hills of negativity, good luck.

July 2, 2019.
Seen the surgeon this morning, bandages are off stitches are gone however I need to keep wearing the sling until the 23rd of this month, so I'll start seeing the physio soon to get some pain free movement in the shoulder area, now it's time to remind the medical professionals, the insurer, my employer and the liaison lady miss X about my forearm, somehow this is becoming an issue that no one wants to know about, I feel very tired with all the running around to get my shoulder injury repaired so I'm going to start all over again try to get my forearm injury repaired.

All the phone calls all the doctor visits, all the referrals, MRI scans, independent assessments, chemists, physio visits, psychologists and so on never ending but it is what it is, I need to get it done so I can be free from this constant pain on my forearm, besides I am not a victim of my own choice I did not choose to injure my shoulder and my forearm at my work place. Anyhow the rest of the day and night some part of my mind is constantly occupied with all of the above as well.

July 3, 2019.
Again not in the mood today to think about anything or write about anything, feeling very flat, I have no interest in anything what soever, day and night blank, blank, blank.

July 4. 2019.
Up and out of bed at 2.30 this morning, having extra coffees and cigarettes, not in a good space at all. Meeting at my workplace today with three of the senior officials miss X the liaison lady and a lady from the union that I'm a member of, the meeting primarily was about how to get me back to work and how soon to get me back to work with no consideration about my mental state no consideration about my physical well being, even though I made a strong point about my left forearm and that it needs to be repaired it was almost ignored and it felt like the idea of getting my forearm repaired was pushed aside that we deal with it when the time comes, actually the union lady made a good point about these people pushing me to return to work without any clearances from my medical treaders was useless there for one and half hours of this meeting was totally useless, the duration of this meeting was intimidating and painful, the eagerness of these people pushing me to return to work where I am medically, physically and mentally not ready has no benefit or advantage to my employer what so ever.

I think the only advantage here is for the insurer to make me return to work no matter how I feel so they can dump me on to my employer and in such a short time my employer can dump me out on the street and then they can all do high fives and tell each other how great it was to close my case so successfully, the way I'm getting treated I can't help but think of all these scenarios, anyway after the meeting I waited almost an hour for a taxi, by now my blood is boiling I'm coming back home with skin full of shit and in my head so much anger I can feel me getting to a raging point, trying to remain calm so I don't do anything regretful . it's not easy it's not easy at all but hey who do I tell, who would listen to me and who would believe me, anyhow back to the rat race that goes around and around in my head day and night with all this bull shit, towards the end of the night more anti depressants and wait for my head to go numb, well as far as I'm concerned that's exactly what any of those anti depressants do to anybody, it is not a tool to fix any of the issues we're dealing with, yeah it might be a powerful opinion, assumption or revelation but I would challenge anyone that has benefited from any of the anti depressants full stop. Anyway it's just another day I'm dealing and stewing in what appears to be my own misery.

I need to stop right now because I can feel myself getting heightened again and the levels of my frustrations are about to hit the roof, not good this is when I get into the area of ideations and wrong doings, I need to stop!!!! I can feel myself about to lose control, I need to stop!!!!

July 5, 2019.
Again very little sleep last night, got up and out of bed all miserable and f##$ing grumpy trying to stay away from my wife so she doesn't cop any of my shit and if she does I don't do it intentionally and when I do get out of hand it's not pretty that's when I spend a lot of time apologizing with tears in my eyes, today like any other day the pain on my left forearm is really given me a lot of grief it is like a tooth ache just won't go away, oh well just got to put up with it until something is done about it, yeah here we go more time and lots more patience, no other choice.

July 6 and 7, 2019.
Same again another couple of days with lots of pain killers anti depressants and agonizing pain on the left forearm, two days in pyjamas, again two fruitless and useless days, some days I wander

how the hell am I still standing when do I call it a day? When do I say enough is enough, is there a time frame for me to make the decision that I can't do this anymore or is that decision will ever be made for me by some unknown powers, I just don't know what to do with this or where to go with it?

Yeah I can feel myself choking with it at times, well that's all for now I'll just call it a day AGAIN!!! Well I guess THAT'S LIFE hey!!

July 8, 2019.

Well I keep saying another sleepless night, another painful night and another agonizing night I'm sure you're sick of reading about it but on the other hand I'm living it day in day out, and yes I'm sick of living it and I am sick and tired of writing about it all and the way I'm living my life now a day's that's all I seem to have just writing, with me isolating myself within the confined spaces of the house and some small areas of the back yard and distancing myself from fake friends and some family members that I can feel myself developing an agoraphobia.

Oh here's something different as I'm walking through a doorway today I knocked my left elbow and my left shoulder into the door jam, well it wasn't pleasant nor was the screaming ugly words that came out of my mouth, once the pain eased off and once again me sheepishly apologizing to my wife and concentrating on keeping the peace at home at least for her sake, that's because at the moment I'm really not in a good space to give a rats arse about myself, I feel if all in my life is going wrong and bad at the moment there's one thing I'm clear about is that I don't need to drag my wife into my sad, useless and worthless circle.

I think it's quite obvious that my love and respect is above what's been served unfairly to me by some unknown circumstantial powers that the sacred area I have reserved for my wife will never be contaminated nor will it ever be broken, anyway I've seen my family doctor today to get some sleeping pills, I do need some solid night's sleep, some days I make concerted effort to get into my thoughts about my future and try to see some light at the end of my tunnel but no avail, no surprise at all, I'll just keep on tapping into my inner strength to keep on seeing this through until the end, no matter how it ends.

July 9, 2019.

I took some sleeping pills last night before bedtime, even though it was broken sleep here and there but at one stage I think I've had a solid four hours of sleep, not enough need more but hey it was better than nothing, I visited my mum this morning, with my wife driving there and picking me up a couple of hours later, it was okay to get out of the house and see my mum for couple of hours but still I couldn't wait to get home, I can't seem to be comfortable or be at ease when I'm away from home, when I'm home I do stew in my own misery in my own way, still thinking about people how they've turned their backs on me and the irony of how people can whisper sweet nothings into one's ear, I don't think these people know how antagonizing it is and how patronizing it can feel and all this starts the inevitable intimidation so there for I find myself in an area where it's so difficult to control my anger, resistance can almost be useless, but once again tapping into my inner strength I seem to find a way to keep the lid on it again.

Yeah I have mentioned inner strength once or twice before, I think this is one of the tools that I've found is quite helpful, it is one of the powerful tools are not readily available to us or can be given to us by any medical professionals, and I think it is one of those tools that no one can lead us to it or guide us on how to get to it, it is almost a self discovery thing, once you have it you hold on to it, tapping into my inner strength seems to be helping me through my days without any regretful decisions, ideations or irreversible actions yet so far, Hey this is just another day with pain killers, antidepressants and head full of shit, complete let down nowhere to go and no one to turn to, well I guess everyone is dealing with their own issues so maybe I shouldn't be too hard on anybody, One day if and when I get better maybe I will be more vigilante on not letting fake and useless people in and around my circle so that dealing with my misery can be much easier than what it is now.

Chapter 9

July 10, 11, 12,1 and 14, 2019.
Again very flat last few days, being isolated and being very restricted physically, not being able to drive and not being able to do a lot of activities on daily basis and being dependent on my wife for almost ninety percent of what I used to do before surgery, so as the days go by it does add more confirming factor to what I already feel heavily is uselessness and worthlessness and there sets in the mood swings again, yeah again I truly don't want to see anyone or talk to anyone, the bottom line some days is that I just don't know what I want, I am not a control freak but some days I have no control at all in anything I do or want, the physical and mental capability of doing anything is becoming lesser and lesser, some days my mood swings are like when it swings one way it seems to get stuck there wether it's good or bad.

If it's bad I can't seem to swing it back but if it's good I can't seem to hold on to it, but one day I want to be optimistic that I will have the opportunity to be able to use a big part of my inner strength to get me out of all this, in the mean while I'll continue with my pain killers and antidepressants.

Oh by the way I need to give credit where it's due to my son, my brother and a good friend of mine that I've known over forty five years, these good people and their partners have been calling me almost on daily basis to check up on me and see if I'm okay or if I need anything, it does feel good and yes it does deter me away from any ideations even if it's on a small percentage it puts a smile on my face momentarily.

July 15, 2019.
Same old this morning just don't want to go into pain and suffering and being uncomfortable in where I am, anyhow I've seen the psychologist this morning, taxi there and back, I know she asks me a lot of questions in order to establish a solid ground to find some tools to be able to help me, but I feel this is going to be a long and windy road.

I feel the questions there are being asked are not directed to the core of my issues it feels like we're fishing around them, so at the end of my session I find myself returning home with nothing gained and nothing lost, except when I get home I feel sad that I shouldn't be subjected to these sessions, but I need to follow the instructions of my medical professionals so that they also followed their medical procedures that if I do end up putting any of my ideations in action that they are in the clear and at the same time they are earning a great income that satisfies them and let's be honest none of these medical professional know me from a bar of soap so really how can they have respect for me and how can they care for me, well that's another story. And guess what else?

I've seen the psychiatrist this afternoon as well, again taxi there and back total session took about twenty minutes, after the introduction the instructions were take more antidepressants and stay home for at least six months, as I'm leaving, out of curiosity I've asked the receptionist if I was to make an appointment without insurance how much would it cost me, the answer was four hundred dollars a session and that he had bookings weeks and months ahead, wow I thought to myself these professionals are financially creating a wonderful life styles for them self's through peoples mental health issues and yet I'm coming back home totally disappointed, I thought the only tool there was available to me was prescription for more antidepressants, really? anyway back to the same old stewing block with unlimited coffees and cigarettes throughout the afternoon and night.

Wow this really feels like I'm back paddling up shit creek. Tomorrow is another day, keep pushing.

July 16, 2019.

Today just like any other day with optimism I'm patiently waiting for my shoulder to heal and get some strength back, and at the same time constantly suffering with pain on left forearm and four to six times a day I get these spasms on my forearm close to my elbow, the only comfort and relief is to rub the area gently and take more pills, however I have an appointment with work injury doctor tomorrow we'll see what happens.

That's all for now just hanging in there using a lot of my inner strength and mental power trying to do my best not to let it get out of control, so again the rest of the day and night is as usual, unlimited coffees and cigarettes, in mentioning the coffees and cigarettes I'm not trying to entice or encourage others to do the same, this is just me and at the moment coffees and cigarettes are what's giving me comfort and consolation, so for now silently I'll just go along with it .

Chapter 10

July 17, 2019.
Without going too much into it painful and boring night, the highlight of my morning today was to see the work injury doctor to find out what can be done about my left forearm injury, after explaining extensively the pain that I'm suffering I don't know if she misunderstood me or pushed my issue aside hoping that it will go away, all she told me was to use some pain eliminating gel and get some stretchy bandage from the chemist and to cover my forearm with it, again how disappointing, I guess I was hoping to get a referral for MRI scanning to be done to find out what sort of an injury I've received and suffering with.

Well, I have to wait to see how long is it going take me to get my message across without getting excessively angry or upset with anyone that's involved with my case, I think the highlight of this morning's consultation was that the pain on my left forearm was acknowledged, the rest of the day and night as usual coffees and cigarettes, that's the way it is at the moment, just can't help it.

July 18, 2019.
Among pain killers and antidepressants last night I took some sleeping pills it was good it gave me some relief and a little bit more sleep than usual, seen my mum for a couple of hours today, at this time of my life my mum's house is the only place I feel calm and peaceful, because of my love and respect for my mum her house almost feels like a house of worship to me, that's the only place where I seem to find peace and serenity, then back home to my usual routine, that's life.

July 19, 2019.

Highlight of the day today to get out of the house was to get a blood test done, went to my usual clinic at eight am this morning only to find out that they don't do it at these premises anymore so I was referred to another place for Monday morning, well this didn't go down well with me controlling my moods for the rest of the day, it almost feels like my patience and my f*&^ing anger have been tested in the last four months, not much seems to be going smoothly lately, but somehow I'm still hanging in there, no other choice I guess.

July 20,21 and 22, 2019.

Not much happening in the last couple of days, just the usual misery, coffees and cigarettes, whatever I'm doing I'm doing it silently in my own confined space without bothering anyone or being bothered by anyone, anyhow went for a blood test this morning and then back home for another useless and worthless day where I have no interest in anything at all, another day with nothing in the horizon, another day of heightened anger and another day of being on the treadmill of self destruction, another day of not being able to find good distraction to deter me away from my usual misery so towards the end of the evening all this results me finding a safe corner in the back yard and start crying like a little boy for a while, well tomorrow is another day, I will face it reluctantly.

July 23, 2019.

Apart from all the usual and miserable night and start to my day I've had a physio session this morning which was very mild, it was the beginning of trying to get some movement and strength into my left shoulder area, it was okay it was enough to give me some positive attitude that at least physically getting better is something that I can look forward to.

Had a long conversation with miss X the liaison lady this morning, it was all about return to work arrangements and forms that she emailed to me, mind you while this is happening with miss

X I have taken off the sling from my arm first time since the surgery, never mind no respect and no duty of care or understanding from miss X obviously escalated the levels of my anger again where I find myself in an uncontrollable rage again, once again I find myself powerless in the hands of these people with the confirmation of feeling useless and worthless, and yes this does push me deeper into the area where I'm already struggling to get out of, well maybe someday, somehow somebody will come along and give me a helping hand to pull me out of this darkness, yeah one would hope.

July 25,25 and 26, 2019.
I wasn't in a good space last couple of days, going through the same usual hurtful, miserable and unhappy thoughts I just couldn't find any energy within myself to write about anything, however seen the physio today, it was okay I'm starting to get some movement in the left shoulder area but the forearm is still giving me a lot of grief, physio lady put some cream on my left forearm and some bandage.

I know this is just a temporary pain relief just like a bandaid, the frustrating thing is that I can't stress it enough or explain it properly that there's definitely something is not right with my left forearm, the ignorance of medically involved people about my left forearm is getting me so bloody angry that I contemplate on doing something so drastic, it gives me an insatiable thirst for blood that it diverts me away from my everyday misery and onto entertaining the idea of hurting people in so many different ways, it takes me a while to turn off away from these terrible thoughts and once I do sometimes it almost feels safe to be stewing in my misery, sometimes I think that maybe I shouldn't reveal too much but at the same time I want to be honest with what goes on in my day to day life as clearly as I can to put it all onto these pages.

July 27 and 28, 2019.
Not a nice couple of days again, low self esteem, no diligence, no integrity, no balance and no direction, just another weekend, it really feels like there's no future, very heavy on insecurity and nothing on the horizon, the BIG question looming above my head

that becomes stormy and thundery is wether to swim or sink? No f^*#ing idea.

July 29, 2019.
Had another session with the psychiatrist this afternoon, it wasn't too bad today we spoke about how I feel and what makes me sad and angry, do I still have suicidal ideations, and because some people at my work place are responsible for me feeling the way I do mentally the psychiatrist told me not to go near my work place for at least three months and told me to continue with the anti depressants, and that I should try and think about all the negative in my head as little as possible yeah easy said than done, taxi there and back.

The rest of the day and night as usual same old same old, excessive amounts of coffees and cigarettes, just can't help myself. Being miserable and staying miserable seems to be the new joy and favoured ways to see my days and nights through.

July 30, 2019.
Not a big day today, I've seen the surgeon at Richmond for a check up, very short consultation, he was happy how the left shoulder progressively recovering and that he'll need to see me one more time, taxi there and back and the rest of the day same old same old.

July 31, 2019.
Today I made an appointment to see my family Doctor to get a referral to get an MRI scan done for my left forearm, I was asked to do this by the work injury doctor, when I try to explain that my family doctor is not involved in work injury matters I was told to just try.

Sure enough I got told by my family doctor that they do not practise work injury matters at all, so I have to go back to work injury doctor again and try to get a referral and than an approval from the insurer to get the MRI scan done on my left forearm, wish me luck, god only knows how long this is going to take, again for the rest of the day and night without going into it, just as usual same old same old.

August 1, 2019.

Restless night again, throughout the night trying to settle the pain on left forearm with pain killers, it's just another thing I'm getting used to, being a pain killer junkie, anyway seen the work injury doctor today together with miss X the liaison lady, yeah finally we concentrated on my left forearm I did receive the referral for an MRI scans and now I'll be chasing the insurer for an approval, we'll see how long that will take.

Today in the afternoon I've received a phone call from miss X asking me to sit with her and the OHS manager to find out what escalates my anxiety and depression levels and to get a second opinion about my mental health issues with one of her colleagues from her office, I told her that I will let her know. when I got home I thought about this for a while, with all the medical professionals on my case that she has my consent to get any information she needs, why would I sit with new people to go all over my mental issues that's been given me so much grief all this time? So yes this makes me wonder if this is lack of professionalism or justification for their employment?

One will never know, it would be easier for these professionals to treat us if they had some firmness in their knowledge and profession. As the days goes by I'm faced with issues like these from half educated professionals that makes it extremely hard to fight the resistance to exist not easy at times, anyway the conclusion to put my mind at ease I will get in touch with my lawyer and a member of the union tomorrow, for now I'll reserve the rest of the afternoon and night to my usual activities Coffees and cigarettes and continue to keep the lid on as best as I can, even though it scares me so much I need to keep on using whatever the power I have to stay safe and the safety of some useless acquaintances does become a major concern in my head, I am not in favour of entertaining these dangerous ideations but sometimes I just can't control it.

August 2, 2019.

Same old very little sleep last night, thinking about miss X's proposal about second opinion, so I called my lawyer and the member of the union and informed them of what was happening and they both advised me against it, so therefore I've called miss X and informed her that I'm not comfortable in getting a second opinion about my mental state and that any proposals in future to be made in writing so she agreed and we left it at that.

Seen the physio this afternoon, more work on left shoulder and the left forearm, left shoulder is starting to get a bit more movement, it's good, bit hopeful, and working on the injured forearm that needs to be repaired is making me uncomfortable and it sure does increase the pain levels to a point where I need more pain killers, if the medical professionals and the insurer that's on my case acted a bit more swiftly all this physical pain and suffering can go away much much sooner, one would think.

Anyway I haven't been writing much about what I go through on daily basis, it's just that I'm truly sick and tired of it all, I want to get over all this shit, I want my life back in order again, I've just about had enough of all this, at times I really do feel like a wild animal that's been caged for so long, I need to be released not break my way out of the cage.

August 3, 2019.

Very restless night again, especially with my left forearm because of yesterdays physio session where she over manipulated the aggravation that the pain on the left forearm escalated to the point where it was almost ten out of ten, but with extra pain killers and perseverance I've seen the night through again with extra coffees and cigarettes, so when the morning comes and the sun rises once again I find myself walking around like a zombie, but hey nowadays that's nothing unusual.

Again it puts me into a situation where I don't want to have anything to do with anyone, I don't want to feel sorry for myself but I can't help feeling sad for where I am at the moment, not to mention anger and a few teary moments here and there, again that's life, as long as I keep myself isolated, with a bit of luck I'll keep myself safe and away from any wrong doings.

August 4, 2019.
Similar to yesterday morning except today the anger levels are higher than usual, I'd like to say I don't know why but then again the painful thoughts and the dangerous ideations never leaves my head I don't get a break from them at all, so I will leave it here for now, not in the right mood and the space I'm in at the moment feels very tight, struggling to breathe, I just can't believe how real this is and how riveting it is.

August 5, 2019.
Today I don't want to talk about how my night was, I don't want to rekindle any emotions to a point of reigniting and going through the same old shit all day if I can help it. So this morning I've decided to walk to the shops to get my prescription, played tatts lotto and I brought a bunch of flowers for my wife just to cheer her up a bit and to apologize for being an absolute and an unreasonable arsehole to her and that she definitely don't deserve all the shit I've been putting her through, and then slowly disappeared into the back yard with my cigarettes where I find a quiet corner to sit and try to climb out of this cold, lonely and dark place where I spend so much time in.

I don't have any optimism at the moment, and even if I did it would be in a misty blurriness in a distance that I would not have the ability to go near it.

August 6, 2019.
Physio again today, she worked on the left shoulder again it is starting get better even if it's on a very low percentage, I guess the situation with my left shoulder can only get better and better from here on, but with the left forearm I don't know I feel we have a long way to go, I'll just wait patiently and keep on pushing with the insurer and the work injury doctor to get referrals and approvals as swiftly as possible, so therefore if not mentally at least physically I can be free from pain and suffering.

I received a phone call from miss X today telling me that she has changed the work injury doctor appointment from twenty-second to twenty-first of this month, yeah that was it no concern about my well being, strictly talking about how soon she can get me back to work.

August 7, 2019.

Today is the day for an MRI scan on my left forearm, great I thought when I left home, so when I arrived they prepared me to go into the scanning machine however the preparation was me being put on a bit of an angle laying on my left putting a lot of pressure on my left shoulder I kept quiet about this.

   I thought I need this done today, I need my left forearm to be repaired so I should and I will put up with the pain, however this was meant to be a thirty minute procedure but I could only last maximum ten minutes.

   My left forearm was placed half under on the side of my body so with some weight on it the pain escalated to the maximum level minute by minute where I could not endure it any further so I asked them to stop scanning and get me out of the machine, I was told that there was another twenty minutes to go, oh boy the pain was so intense as I was leaving the clinic I felt myself starting to get heightened, I was absolutely furious that if there was someone near me that I disliked I don't think that I would have been responsible for my actions, with this rage in me I could have done some serious damage to someone or someone's property, I don't know what held me back, I don't know how I managed to calm down, maybe I've tapped into my inner strength maybe I'm a lot stronger than I give myself credit for.

   I am ever so thankful that I arrived home in one piece, and when I did get home to confirm my calmness the immediate thing to do was to have three short black coffees and about six cigarettes, and when I did get my composure back I informed miss X and the insurer so I can get another approval for an MRI at another date, I did not mentioned me been in a rage to miss X or the insurer, so the rest of the day and night well I did go through some period there where I found my chest becoming a bit tight and having difficulties breathing, no it isn't from excessive amount of coffees or cigarettes, it is from using excessive amounts of strength to contain myself and refrain myself from dangerous actions. Well tomorrow is a new day I hope I have a better one.

Chapter 11

August 8, 2019.
Terrible night last night, even though I took sleeping pills and the antidepressant at about six pm I just wanted to knock myself out no pain and no headache I thought but it didn't work about ten pm consisting pain on left forearm where it dictated me to take more pain killers, total of about three hours of sleep. Out of bed this morning with low level of pain on left shoulder and heavy pains on the left forearm, and the head?

I don't know how to put it in words, I feel like I'm a caged animal I want to rip someone's head off, I want to take someone apart and when the urge wears off I find myself in the corner somewhere trying to hold my tears back, I don't know what these antidepressants are doing to me, they are supposed to help me with my emotions and bring my head to happy medium well I don't know about that but I'll keep taking them to see what happens.

August 9, 2019.
Just one of those days today where I don't seem to have energy for anything, I feel my tolerance levels are right down, very flat and blank for just about anything, I have no interest in anything, no care factor for whatever happens around me, just sad and teary, oh boy days like today are so long and so lonely, it's one of those days that if I was surrounded by a thousand people I would still feel alone, yeah well I can feel that it's going to be a long day and night. I wish myself all the best to cope and keep it together.

August 10 and 11, 2019.
Same again last night, pain killers, sleeping pills and antidepressants I still don't believe that antidepressants are working at all, I don't understand, well here's the scenario I have a lot of issues I'm dealing with at the moment, what I have is all in my head, it's all mental so therefore I have a lot of issues I'm dealing with at the moment, what I have is all in my head, it's all mental so therefore my issues in my head brings my confidence, my strength and my self esteem right down so drastically that this is not physical it's mental so how the hell can a little pill called antidepressant bring my mental status back in f*&^ing order, it is not f*&^ing physical !!

I personally have come to a very strong assumption that no one knows how to fix it, it's all trial and error. There's nothing concrete, I've heard from the professionals telling me take these antidepressants if they don't work come back and we'll give you something different, Really? I have spoken to some people who are in a similar situation as I am and none of us have any solutions we're all walking around like zombies, yeah this only confirms it to me again that there are only pills and words available for us no solid tools at all, and at the end of the day we all have a choice I'm sure I don't need to verbalize this. I don't know how to be more simpler, yeah I write about all this, I'm experiencing it and I'm living it day after day, the days and nights are long, being isolated this is the only thing I can do at the moment, is Just Write.

Oh just before I go one thing I found out about the antidepressant that I'm on at the moment, it's called valdoxan, I've been prescribed this pill by the work injury doctor and the psychiatrist and the side effects are that if I want to hurt myself or want to commit suicide that the feelings gets worse in the first few weeks, yes that's true I've experienced that but if that's a fact why the hell is this pill been prescribed to us?

Again at the end of the day is it all about the money? You see, the Thierry with the majority of the medical professionals is that if the patient is still with us after three to four weeks of prescribing the antidepressant we'll either go to plan B which none of them have or we'll just keep on prescribing the antidepressants for how long it takes, hey at the end of the day medical professionals aren't cheap, they get paid handsomely and most importantly all us sufferers are just another number to these professionals, I would stand to be corrected wrong.

August 12, 2019.

Yeah got up this morning nothing different, few cigarettes and few coffees later went to get the MRI scan done on my forearm for the second time, yeah they prepared and placed me into a little hole, what was supposed to be thirty minutes it ended up been one and a half hours, yes it did get uncomfortable and yes it did become excessively painful on left shoulder and left forearm and again it does trigger the mental part once again trying hard not to let it get out of hand, however it got done, so when the results come through I will be seeing an independent Doctor for a physical assessment in the city on Thursday the fifteenth.

I am following every instruction from everyone that's on my case, once I see the independent examiner we'll see how long it will take for the insurer to make the decision to give me an approval to get the surgery done on my left forearm, this is where lots and lots of patients needed while coping with pain and mental instability, it's not easy living with the idea of knowing being misunderstood and being ignored, That's life it's a brand new era for me that I have to learn to live with it.

August 13, 2019.

Don't want to write about any of the usual stuff today where it does reignite issues in my head, however more to the positive side I've seen the physio this morning, we are making progress with my left shoulder, I am able to lift my left arm a little bit higher, even though it became painful at times I am trying to get the full usage of my left arm or at least close to maximum capacity, well the rest of the day and night what can I say that I haven't said so many times before.

August 14, 2019.
Had a meeting this morning at my workplace with miss X, OHS manager and the lady from the union, when I got up this morning knowing about the meeting and the idea of facing these people was enough to trigger my mind and get heightened a little bit, however with my shoulder not being recovered from the surgery yet and the pain on my left forearm I did attended the meeting, again it was all about how soon can I get back to work and with no concern of my physical well being or my mental at the moment.

After some fruitless discussions and me having some firm and heavy input almost losing my cool the union lady addressed the fact to miss X and the OHS manager that until I get clearances from the doctor and the psychiatrist that these sorts of meetings were useless and unnecessary, so the meeting was a total waste of time for us all, one good thing came out of it is that until I get clearances and I'm back at my full capacity both mentally and physically that they won't burden me with the idea of sending me back to work, it's not that I don't want to return to my employment, more than physical I don't think that I'm mentally ready yet, with some of the deep and dangerous thoughts I have I strongly believe that I should be kept away from my workplace, I'll write about these dangerous thoughts one day when I build enough confidence, not today not ready yet.

August 15, 2019.
Absolutely a terrible night I had again last night, shoulder pain combined with forearm pain and quite a number of toilet visits and vomiting, not good not much sleep at all and not much energy this morning, however got up got dressed and went to the city for an independent medical examination which I thought it was useless and totally unnecessary but I got to do what I got to do follow instructions from every f&^%ing direction, that's life it's all a money grabbing exercise from all these organizations, it appears to be a sad and cunning way of making money, but that's the way it is just follow the rules, you can't change the world but the world has a mysterious ways of changing you, just except it, gets easier if

you do, anyway the reason for the medical examiner visit today was to find out how the recovery on my left shoulder is progressing and based on the report the insurer can make the final decision to send me back to work.

When I was being examined with the limited movement that I couldn't move my left arm at the doctors request he started to move his head side to side and asked me why did the insurer send you here, you seem to have a long way to go, so the whole consultation was about five minutes, so you can understand my anguish and why I get so angry, starting to feel like a football between medical professional where I get handballed a lot, so there are profitable benefits are been made, good on you heartless people I keep thinking, thinking like this is one of the side effects of being constantly angry.

Again I came home with all these thoughts not being able to help it it's one pm now hoping to have an easy afternoon and night, I can't eat anything the stomach hasn't settled yet, but it won't stop me from having coffees and cigarettes, so here I go again back into the rut I can feel it's going to be a long afternoon and a long night again.

August 16, 2019.

Not much to write about today not in the mood to do anything vary flat, lots of heavy breathing and a few teary moments, that's all for today.

Chapter 12

August 17, 2019.
It's a sad day today for me and my wife, two years ago today we've lost a very dear and very special friend of ours, my wife and I got a bit teary remembering how wonderful she was especially with my wife, they were close almost like sisters, spoke to my friend yesterday he assured me that he will come and visit me today but it didn't happen oh well, quite day and quite night nothing exciting .

August 18, 2019.
Quite day and night last night, there's not much to write about today, except with all that's going around and around in my head that I'm starting to feel that I'm running on empty, I'm feeling that I'm using the last bit of my reserved energy, the heavy pain on my forearm running all the way down to my fingers is not helping my mood at all.

I keep thinking that this is all going to get better one day, I keep thinking and trying to believe in hope, whatever the hope is these days, I wish I could find a way to be enthusiastic

August 19, 2019.
Late yesterday afternoon I had very heavy pain from my left shoulder all the way down to my hand and fingers with pins and needles, spasms that it was almost unbearable, thank heavens for the pain killers, apart from all that pain and physical suffering I'm still trying to be strong on faith and trying to have patience that it will be a smooth sailing one day and at the same time I'm still reluctant to put on these pages as to what goes through my mind,

it actually scares me if it comes out in the open one day it may be held against me in the court of law, I don't want to end up behind bars or some mental institute or worse six foot under.

However one day I will find the courage to write more on how I really feel without being fearful, anyway that's all for now, head down stay isolated so I can stay out of trouble.

August 20, 2019.
Seen the physio this morning, careful and limited workout on left shoulder and restrictions put on my left forearm by me, I strongly believe that there's something not right with my left forearm that no physio or no amount of pain killers will ever fix the problem without surgery, throughout this ordeal as I've mentioned before that I know I've lost associating with some friends and some family members where I thought we were close, yeah some of them came to visit me, it was such a quick visit that when they left the coffee cups were still warm, the fake and useless friends and family members I've lost that sometimes I wonder if we were friends to begin with, one will never know, one must keep on pushing shit uphill if one wants to survive.

Oh thank god for the couple friends we have that lives up north of Melbourne we've known them forever, they check up on me genuinely and constantly so I won't give up on humanity just yet

August 21, 2019.
Seen the injury doctor and miss X this morning, the doctor received the MRI results and that I might need a surgery done on my left forearm, so far the good thing about this is that it's been revealed that I wasn't faking my injuries that there's genuinely some damage done to my left shoulder and my left forearm at work, so now I need to organize another surgeon for my left forearm as if I don't have enough shit going through my head, however while all this happening miss X is doing her absolute best to get me back to work under my current situation, wow talk about being dedicated to her profession miss X comes across ruthless, heartless and totally unprofessional no compassion at all, but that's another story that I

need to pay less attention to so I don't have her under my radar as well, and the injury doctor has given me stronger pain killers, so now I have three different pain killers from three different doctors where this almost confirms my theory about assumption of a lot of things, so what chance do a lot of people with mental health issues have.

The bottom line is that our so called medical professionals might not have any idea and sometimes they make us feel like guinea pigs and get paid top dollar for it, I hope I'm not offending anyone by thinking like this and writing it all down on these pages, in a strange way it does help me go through the sad and lonely days and nights, yeah talking about sad, dark, lonely and no way out feelings never take a break they never have a rest, I just go through with it day in day out, never mind that's my problem I'll deal with it.

August 22, 2019.

Spoke to someone from the insurance company today, she's going to organize an authorisation form for me to see an elbow surgeon and she made it clear to me that this will be a consultation just to find out what needs to be done, knowing what the insurance companies are like and this conversation had some negative feel to it I guess I just have to wait to see how long will I be suffering before I get some positive results about how soon I can have my left forearm injury repaired, I'm getting sick of hearing that I should put some cream on my forearm and take pain killers for the last six years.

August 23, 2019.

Not much is happening, nothing for the weekend, just the usual boring TV, cigarettes and coffee's, so today I just want to put down my thoughts about " Time Heals' well I have totally different opinion about this, time heals nothing, it's what we've been told for many years to give us some kind of hope, comfort or peace, it really doesn't help with any of it at all, in fact with each individual dealing with their own mental or physical issues can allow themselves become either a little kitten or a big roaring Lyon, feeling like a little kitten can mean that you've lost all hope, you feel useless you feel worthless you have a very low self esteem and that you're at the understanding and excepting that this is the way to live not much you can do about it, worst case scenario is that one day you will pull the plug and end it all so therefore time does not heal, time does nothing, in this period us as humans we explore avenues we entertain some thoughts good or bad who is to judge us or who are we to judge anyone.

So time goes by without discrimination or prejudice, on the other hand let's talk about the time turning us into a Lion. Yeah time and the unpleasant circumstances that we find ourselves in can easily turn us into Lions, and when that happens last thing you can think of is how time can heal, what we really think about is why are we here? How did we get here? and most importantly who put us here? These are all important questions.

We're all human some of us except the circumstances differently and with some of us we may have this insatiable hunger for revenge that it wasn't our choice or our fault we found ourselves in, where we are, so we have this powerful need to hold these people responsible and make them pay for what they've done to us, it is human nature we just can't help it, so yes this is when we find ourselves in a rage where we roar like a Lion, so my theory is that time dose not heal, it can really turn some of us into monsters, in fact I feel my blood boiling right now, my chest is getting tighter my breathing is getting heavier, I simply want to hurt some people badly beyond recognition, I want some people to pay for what they've done to me, you see I don't want to be sitting here and writing all about my negative and dangerous thoughts, I just want my life back before the injuries where life was good and I could handle anything, and now it feels like a constant struggle and time is not healing anything at all.

Time is only creating opportunities for some of the dangerous thoughts I've explored and entertained in my head but not yet actioned, and the opportunities we create often comes with some unacceptable consequences where it pulls us back from actioning some of the final activities that can give our family members full of sorrow or full of regrets that they all misunderstood us, so therefore time may change our direction into our future and give us a chance to put all the hurt and suffering behind us but time will never heal what we've gone through, well that's my opinion and my assumption I've made over the years, I'm not about to change my mind, and here comes the phrase we all hate hearing " everything is going to be alright" quite unknown isn't it?

August 26, 2019.

Hey just another ordinary night last night, limited sleep again on and off no big drama I guess I'm getting used to it, anyway had a good old chat with the psychologist this morning about a few things, I assured her that I had no intentions of hurting myself or others but at the same time I told her that I have this desperate need to hold some people accountable for my situation I'm in now.

I'm not sure how she took that but she'll let me know next time I see her, I'm under the impression that she will get in touch with my psychiatrist and miss X about the unjustly manifested forms by miss X for me to get back to work before I get my head in a right state, I would like to write more today but I feel the need to cut it short, what I really do like to reveal might be out of line, maybe in the next few months when I build enough courage, but for now back to my coffees and cigarettes best combination to keep me calm we'll see what tomorrow brings.

August 27, 2019.

Had a physio appointment this morning at 9.30 am but it's cancelled my physio called in sick so the new appointment is on Saturday at 9.30 am, I have seen the psychiatrist this afternoon I've asked him to fill in the forms from Miss X he was happy to do it but I don't think he wants to communicate with her at all.

Anyway after speaking with him and answering few of his questions he told me that he doesn't think I'll be ready for any employment between six to twelve months, so he will be treating me on regular basis same as the psychologist so I have sessions with both of them until December at least, in the mean while I'm heavily concentrating on full recovery of my left shoulder and waiting to see what happens with my left forearm injury, there seems to be no hurry with the insurer so I just got to sit back and wait patiently, it does get very frustrating, it almost feels as if the insurer doesn't see my pain so it's not there it doesn't exist, so the rocky road ahead becomes even more rockier waiting for referrals and approvals from both the insurer and the medical practitioners.

In the mean while everything else is still the same with pain killers and antidepressants, quite often when I sit outside early hours of the morning in the dark one hour feels like one day so much goes through my mind, I seem to use a lot of strength trying to keep the lid on and control the pilot light not letting it ignite, not easy.

August 28, 2019.

I know I'm going to mention I've had another restless night, pain running up and down from my left shoulder down to my hand I know it gets boring at times that I keep repeating but this is real, this is what happens just about every day and every night.

Anyway I spoke to my lawyer this morning about my super fund not being contributed, she assured me that it was all above border line, and that she is preparing a case not only for common law claim for pain and suffering but for harassment from my manager and for bullying from one of my team members so I guess hearing this that something is getting done by a professional was reassuring for me that I had someone on my side, someone that hears me and listens to me, also had a chat with Miss X today about yesterdays outcome with the psychiatrist, I don't think she was happy, the answers to her questioner from the psychiatrist was not satisfactory, I think it put a big hurdle in her path that she can't get me back to work quick enough, we will have a further discussions about it on Wednesday when we see the work injury Doctor.

I know Miss X is only doing her job to the best of her ability but with her unprofessional and immature attitude without realizing she can push me to the brink of losing my cool, thank goodness I'm doing my best to keep it under control. So I guess so far so good that I haven't shot anyone or ripped anyone's head off, I'm doing okay, I just don't want any bull shit reason or any poor excuse, that's it for now back to managing my aches and pains and my mind to the best of my ability, I keep promising myself that I will not lose it and to stay in control best way I can.

August 29, 2019.

Last night before I went to bed I decided to be strong, see the night through without pain killers yeah the pain was there the urge not to take pain killers was over powering, so when I got out of bed early this morning I felt a bit invigorated, hoping that I can do it again tonight, today my wife took me to my mum's for a couple of hours, it was good seeing my mum, I guess the rest of the day and night will be as usual, oh if you're ever in doubt, down and just about out I hope you have someone that can come along to listen and understand you and respect you, god only knows you going to need that person, Good luck.

August 30, 2019.

Got up this morning as usual aching shoulder and forearm, thinking there's not going to be much happening today, I also feel the head is full of shit, so it feels as I've already made the assumption that I'll be stewing about all the miserable shit that's in my head all day and all night again, 11.50 pm guess what? I just came inside to write about what I predicted would happen today has happened and continuing, I just wish there was a way out of it, yeah maybe there are ways out of it all, I don't mean the wrong choices, I just want to snap out of it and get back to a normal life again.

I'm not ready to make that last choice yet, I'm still hoping it won't come to finalizing it once and for all, I guess this is another way of saying that the pilot light never goes out, about the pilot light sometimes I wonder if there's anyone out there that knows what I'm talking about.

August 31, 2019.
Seen the physio this morning, a new person, apparently my usual physio is on annual leave, so this new person trying to start me on heavy pulling, pushing and lifting, with my left shoulder been operated less than two months ago and my left forearm is yet to be operated on, not long after we started.

I got up and asked him politely to stop and that I will wait for my usual physio to return from annual leave and then I will return, I've made a new appointment and left the clinic, I've asked my wife to take me to my mum's for a couple of hours, it was good to spend some quality time with my mum it feels like best medicine at times.

Chapter 13

September 1, 2019.

The day is extra sad and miserable today, my son is overseas and my daughter is in interstate, not much of a father's day, on top of that I can see my wife is starting to show signs of sadness and hurt about my current situation this doesn't sit too well with me, I don't want her to witness any of the shit I'm going through, she doesn't deserve any of it, I truly don't want to lose her through all this misery that I'm going through, without her in my life the consequences would absolutely be devastating.

I know one thing that I won't be in control of my actions, I know one thing for sure that I'm just holding on, ready to F^*#ing snap. My wife offered me an opportunity today to take me out for breakfast, lunch or dinner for father's day, but unfortunately I refused bluntly, not in the mood and definitely not in the right state of mind at the moment, I'm a very lucky man that I have loving and respectful wife that understands and excepts where I am at the moment.

September 3, 2019.

Not much happened yesterday except I decided to go to the shopping mall with my wife and I told her that I'll give it a go driving there, it was only about five kilometres from where we live, it was okay getting there but my wife drove us back, for some reason I found it hard to concentrate and I was struggling to focus, so back home to the same old at least I gave it a try I thought so when the sun started to rise this morning, after spending considerable amount time outside in the back yard with my ever so faithful coffees and cigarettes that kept me company, now I thought I'll give driving another try and go to my mum's on my own, mum lives' about twenty kilometres from my house so worst case scenario I'll pull over and get a taxi back I thought, so I thought this was a good idea to get me out of the house and a good opportunity to start getting around to get me out of my misery.

I thought, anyway three quarters of the way to my mum's I had to pull over, because when I made a left hand turn I've used my left arm a bit more than I should have, so therefore the pain not only on my left shoulder and my left forearm but on my head as well profusely escalated to a level where I had no choice but to pull over and sit there for about twenty minutes and yes I had my cigarettes with me, anyhow after that little ordeal I did manage to visit my mum, but I couldn't get home quick enough and that makes me sad as well thinking that I might be developing an agoraphobia, not happy at all.

September 4, 2019.
Had an appointment to see the work injury Doctor today together with Miss X, I don't why but today they were both gentle with me even if it was fake they've shown me a bit of concern, even though Miss X was concentrating on getting me back to work but she was careful about it, and then towards the end of the consultation one of the questions was do I still want to hurt myself, well!

I've cut it short I couldn't wait to get out of there and get home and when I did made myself a black coffee grabbed my cigarettes and found myself in the back yard where I can get lost in my thoughts, yeah the question I was asked today about self harm was not comfortable with me, it really is an intimidating and down grading question, you can almost feel patronized by this question, I mean instead of giving these medical practitioners an answer whether or not you're going to harm yourself you really want to ask them the question, hey if I do want to harm myself would I tell you about it, do I want to advertise it or do I ask for instructions?

So without realizing our medical practitioners can really push you over the edge and in my strong and invalid opinion is that if a person is going to put suicidal ideations in action there's quite often no preparations are made for it and it certainly becomes the biggest and the final decision and the final choice one would ever make, so it is very hard to answer that question that comes from our medical practitioners, hey chances are I could answer one thing and do something totally different, so there you go, try and not to ask a person that's on the edge the question of whether they will hurt themselves or others, you will never get the desirable answer, as well as a normal person the person that's on the journey of self harm or harm others will always have a hidden agenda, and no matter how good you think you are or how professional you think you are you will never ever put a finger on it and deter them from their ideations or actions, I know this for a fact, it's like when we commit sins or crime no one can know about it, we just go ahead and do it whether it's right or wrong simply because we wouldn't want to give anyone a chance to deter us or try and change our minds, I think what I'm trying to say is that being ignored by the people who are close to us can only feel like a confirmation of how useless and worthless we are.

All we want is that everything can be as normal as they used to be before we were pushed into the state we're in now. And one important thing is that we did not put ourselves into this state we're in now, oh no we're not proud of who we are and where we are now, just struggling to get out of this deep, dark, cold and lonely place where we don't want to be in, simple but hard to do. NO HELP!!!!

September 5, 2019.
Quite day again today not much happening, I keep saying same old same old yeah I'm sick of it too and I know at times I minimize writing about the things happened in the course of twenty four hour day, that's because I don't want to write about the same things there are happening day in day out and keep on living the same misery over and over again but the sad thing about it is that I can't run away from it all, and at times I refuse to write about every single thing goes through my mind, and if I did I probably need up to fifteen or more pages per day.

So far I'd like to think and most importantly believe that I'm dealing with all that's happening the best way I possibly can, as I mentioned once or twice before I'm still reluctant to speak with anyone I just don't have the energy or the patience for it, I am getting used to being ignored so therefore I am dealing with it all silently in my own confined space, thinking there's a lot of uncertainty, feels like there's no future and no hope, I need to stop now I am starting to breath heavy and getting quite emotional again.

September 6, 2019.
Quite day again today, trying not to dwell on anything today, I really have no inspiration to write about any anything, feeling down and very flat. I just don't want to get angry or emotional any more than I already am, I just want to concentrate on getting myself off of the treadmill of self destruction.

September 7, 2019.
I've gone to see my mum this morning, it truly was a struggle to drive there and back, I feel I need to get my confidence levels back up again and my concentration needs to improve, and more strength on my left shoulder and less pain on my left forearm, anyway the rest of the day and night was as usual.

September 8, 2019.
Oh oh here we go again, got up this morning in a fierce rage, I don't know and I don't understand why? I just can't put a finger on it, my wife went to her mums this morning nothing against my wife but I couldn't wait for her to leave, I'm not in the right mood to see or speak to anyone.

I don't know where is this uncontrollable rage is coming from,, in my head right now it feels like there's going to be a violent eruption a wild explosion, I think I'll have a quite day and night today so I don't do anything or say anything to anyone that I might regret for a long long time.

Chapter 14

September 9, 10 and 11, 2019.
Last couple of days I did not want to write about anything at all, just a lot of thinking and agonizing pain in left forearm, left shoulder not too bad at all in fact I am getting a good mobility on the left shoulder I feel that I'm starting to get up to around fifty to fifty five percent usage however I'm still worried and concerned about my left forearm, the insurers are taking their time and doing a good job of keeping me in the dark about any of the procedures at the moment, at the same time I just can't help but think that my left shoulder and my left forearm will never be the same again, taking my age and the way I feel about everything and the certain people around me in to consideration I am not doing too well at the moment.

It is one of those days again and the last two days everything I do everything I see whoever I speak to right now I have no interest I seem to have zero tolerance, this is the third day continues with this burning rage in my head that I'm absolutely petrified not knowing if I can be responsible for my actions, and if I can stand in front of my capabilities and not let anything get out of hand.

I do own some items that can cause some serious damage so therefore yes I am scared and I am worried, I know what I feel I just can't express any of these to anyone in a conversation, only to those who are in the same situation as I am, then again if they are in the same situation as I am they wouldn't want to be talking to anyone as well, so there you go we do suffer in silence, we're only seem to be heard if we action any of the ideations we've been contemplating, even though with the unwarranted, unexplained and useless antidepressants we've been prescribed and we do take them to numb our sculls and walk around like zombies we can still contemplate some unthinkable and unimaginable ideations that we can even shock ourselves at times, wow it must be extremely difficult for medical professionals to exactly identify our mental health problems or categorize us, as most of us may know that there are up to three hundred mental health cases and thirty of them are the main ones just about every one of us know about.

We all know someone that suffers with one out of thirty main mental health cases, some of the examples are Ptsd, depression, paranoia, anxiety disorders, bipolar affective disorder, schizophrenia, panic disorders, eating disorders and the list goes on and on and some of the antidepressants are valdoxan, serotonin, Prozac, celexa, Zoloft, luvox, sertraline and same with these the list goes on and quite a few of these antidepressants have been taken of the market because the side effects were outweighing the benefits, yeah well this does leave a big question in my mind that the antidepressant that I'm taking how beneficial is it to me? The reason I'm paying too much attention to all these is that I don't believe my antidepressants are working on me at all.

Well that's my opinion I guess I'm entitled to it.

September 12, 2019.
Yeah I'm still fuming from last few days, I'm still finding it hard to comprehend that I'm totally misunderstood and misheard, when I say misheard I know that when I speak to any of the medical professionals I get the impression that they know I'm speaking but they don't hear me and they're not listening so therefore it is hard to get serious answers to any of my questions, here I go again my head hurts.

I'm upset and angry and all my focus goes onto the people that have put me here, again all these emotions are turning into a savage revenge, as I keep saying that the pilot light never goes out.

September 13, 2019.
I've had a physio appointment today but I've cancelled it, not in the mood not in the right space, I just can't seem to get myself up and out of this deep and dark place, these feelings are about to break me .

I need more strength and more patience, sometimes I wish I could write everything I truly feel, but now I feel the need to hold back. Maybe one day I will stand up and walk forward, maybe not, at the moment I don't have any answers or any hope at all.

September 14, 2019.
Again last couple of days not much to write about, it feels like my mind is like a mine field, anything I think of is like a mine I've just stepped on, whatever I think of becomes explosive in my head one after another, it really becomes unbearable so in order to stay out of trouble and not hurt anyone I choose to be left alone, I really think it's the safest for the moment, and these useless tablets I'm taking by the order of medical professionals are not helping at all.

I'm just suffering and putting up with these bullshit side effects, constipation, insomnia, weight gain, diarrhoea and so on, with these so called medical professionals making me try all different medication makes me feel like a guinea pig, why don't they give me the right medication in the first place? I'll never know, so it goes waste of time waste of money.

September 16, 2019.
9.00 o'clock appointment this morning with the psychologist, it's hard to understand sometimes if we are achieving anything or where we are going with these visits, we did discuss the report from Miss X about return to work program and the discussions we've had with the work injury Doctor.

I've asked to have a copy of these forms to be emailed to me, I've gone there and back with a taxi that was supplied by the insurer, as I'm writing this now at midday killing some time before my next appointment in Richmond at three pm, so my next appointment in Richmond was an independent psychiatrist examination organized by the insurer to find out how serious my condition is or to find out if I'm faking all this, anyhow with the psychiatrist things got very intense and I got very emotional, some of the questions become highly intimidating, it sure did lifted my anger to maximum levels.

I found myself almost to the point of emotional break down at one stage, and another point emotions got the better of me that I broke down in tears I just couldn't help myself, wow so many questions, we went back as far back as when I was six years old, so it would be interesting to see what kind of a report the insurer will receive from this examiner, hey whatever! I guess I have nothing to hide, I do follow every instruction from each and every medical and non medical professionals including Miss X, my employer and the insurer for more reasons than one, my physical recovery and my mental stability are very important at the moment, so I can get normality back into my life again.

Seeing the examiner this afternoon again with a taxi there and back supplied by the insurer, now early evening what I'm doing at the moment is dusting off and get ready for another session with my useless psychiatrist tomorrow, and again the rest of the night well who knows what it's going to be like, I will face the long lonely and dark night the best way I know how for the moment.

September 17, 2019.
Seen the psychiatrist again this afternoon, it totally was another fruitless consultation, more antidepressants been prescribed and less understanding of what my situation is all about.

I think I get more understanding and more respect from the people who are in the similar situation as I am and very little from highly educated medical professionals, day after day it gets more and more confirmed to me that being ignored is the worst thing anyone can handle let alone if you are suffering with some sort of mental issues, telling someone with mental health problems to be strong, you'll be all right and that it's all in your head is the very last thing they need to hear as they might not have much to hold onto anymore.

We can all offer a lot of support and comfort to those who had minor or major surgeries and help them to recover as quickly as possible but with the ones who are suffering mentally majority of us don't have the knowledge, understanding or education in order to offer them the right tools to help them to get out of that cold, lonely and dark place each and everyone with mental issues are suffering in silence, now what makes me think like this and have a very strong opinion or assumption about some of the medical professionals.

I have had discussions with some people who are in a similar situation as I am and one of them told me that they are doing okay and their counselling sessions are helping them and yet they lose it over something totally unreasonable and they get very heightened very quickly, and I ask them the question of how many sessions they've had and to my shock they tell me that they've had well over forty sessions, well I automatically think that there's a misconduct on financial grounds here from some of these so called medical professionals that they are making a very comfortable living financially out of peoples miseries where they offer no useful tools at all, the only two tools they offer is antidepressants and meditation, Really? When I'm heightened.

I'm full of rage and I have some dangerous ideations meditation is the last thing I would really give a rats arse about. Anyhow in the process of mental and physical recovery I do spend a lot of time at home, this is one of the reasons why I'm able to put whatever goes through my mind on these pages, and averaging four hours of sleep out of twenty four hours in a day it does keep my thoughts awake with me whether they good or dangerous, well that's life another evening and maybe another long night ahead.

September 2 and 22, 2019.
Last few days I just been out of it, just couldn't be bothered about thinking, talking or doing anything, I know and except that it can be damaging the communications with my close family members and my social life well not much of that at the moment, I just don't have any care factor at the moment It's absolute zero, I don't do it

on purpose, yeah I keep hearing things will get better and don't give up on hope, well how can you give up on hope when you think you have no hope at all, this I might understand one day, but for now I'm trying to keep up with all my appointments without losing my cool.

I feel that I'm coming to a breaking point more easily and more often now. I know I need to keep going without doing something that might be unforgiving . Best of luck, god only knows I need it

September 23, 2019.
Seen the psychologist this morning, she's done a fifteen minute relaxation session or meditation with me, while this was happening there was a kid outside in the waiting area running around and making a lot of noise, when the meditation ended after fifteen minutes she asked me if it helped and was it beneficial, I told her that I was distracted and I got very angry with the kids parents and that I almost lost control and she told me that we might try it again next time if it's quieter, and yeah for that I arrived home with some anger.

The rest of the afternoon and night well here it is again same old same old. Oh before I forget it's my birthday today it's the big sixtieth and my wife organized one of my friend and his brand new partner to come over for my birthday and they did, and nothing unusual they couldn't wait to leave my house, oh well at least I had someone over for my big birthday, nothing important at the moment I just thought I'll mention it, yeah it is sad if I wasn't going through what I'm going through right now I could've had a gathering of up to sixty people for my big birthday, oh well just another day I guess.

September 24, 2019.
Seen the physio this morning, she was happy with the progress I'm making and I'm comfortable with her treatment she is gentle and thorough.

From there not much else the boring sentence again for the rest of the day and night here it is same old same old.

September 28 and 29, 2019.
Again not much to write about the last few days, continuing with the pain killers I've received from three different Doctors, at the moment I'm too anxious to see what can be done about my left forearm as I am seeing a new surgeon early next month.

The left shoulder is still giving me a bit of grief as I still don't have full reach in any direction with my left arm and my left forearm well I now know for a fact that it surgically needs to be repaired, no two ways about it, now with the physical side of my issues as well as the mental instability not that I want to talk about it but I can truly feel that all this is having an impact on my marriage and obviously my social life.

It really scares me that if my wife comes to a point that she's had enough of my miserable existence well that's when the inevitable will take place, I feel the need to stop right here right now, I feel I'm getting heightened again, I can't even look at anyone at the moment let alone communicating, I need to end it now so I can go outside and get some air, I'm having difficulties breathing.

October 1, 2019.
Restless night again, because I can't sleep on my left side trying to lay on my back or on my right side for long periods is not working it really gets annoying to the point where I lose sleep, not good and not comfortable but not much I can do about it.

Life goes on and it must, anyhow seen the Surgeon this morning he made me do some movements with my left shoulder and my left forearm' difficult and painful at times and we spoke about me driving he suggested that I don't drive just yet he felt it wasn't safe for me to drive my manual ute however he said I can drive an automatic car at my discretion if I feel safe to do so, he wants to see me again on the tenth of December, taxi there and back again.

So back home, back to my isolation again the one that's unintentionally been created for me, I just can't seem to be able to control the issues in my head and drifting into my sad and sometimes dangerous thoughts until the early hours of the morning, I don't do it on purpose and I certainly don't enjoy it but at the moment I just don't have the ability to stop it by any means at all, yeah it's a worry, tomorrow is another day we'll see what happens.

October 2, 2019.
Seen the work injury Doctor today, based on the independent psychiatrist report and my ongoing appointments she's given a non capacity form for another one month, and we spoke about the medication that I'm on and I found she struggled to explain it to me how the medication works and how the pills were made and what was used to make some of these pills.

Well as long as she prescribes to me and I take them so therefore we will all be happy, so we think or believe and whichever way it works or not I guess it is up to each individuals prerogative, with everything else very short and blank today.

I'm just not in any mood to expose what's in my head, again shortness of breath, my head feels like it has a physical pain from all the issues that I'm struggling to deal with, it's constant and it hurts, just another day and possibly a long and another fearful night.

October 4, 2019.
Walked to physio this morning, it was a bit of an outing away from my usual confined and miserable environment, anyway the physio was good she made me do some different movements today to get some strength back into my left shoulder and even though it was useless she worked on my left forearm with no satisfactory benefit at all.

I mean let's be honest my left forearm has incurred an injury at the same time as my left shoulder so therefore it would be fair to believe that it definitely needs surgical repairing one would think, but it has become one of my new policies that I don't want to argue or go against any of the professionals that are treating me at the moment.

I do give a lot of credit to the physio that she is dedicated to her profession and she is doing her best to help me recover, and the rest of the day today, tonight and the weekend will be as per usual nothing on the agenda, yeah again I need to keep the lid on, I need to try and keep my head clear of and away from some of the things that I want to do are definitely not safe and don't want to elaborate on anything right now, I am in fear of getting myself in trouble.

I'm okay, I'm okay, I'm okay, I keep repeating to myself, I want to believe that I will get my genuine happiness back one day, It's getting harder and harder to keep on pretending that everything is okay, It really is not easy to keep the one's I love to worry less.

Chapter 15

October 7, 2019.
I've seen a new surgeon this morning In Richmond about my left forearm injury, he told me that surgery on my left forearm was not needed at this point and he gave me some forms to give to my physio to continue the treatment on my left forearm and for me to continue taking pain killers when necessary and for me to consider couple of cortisone injections and after two or three months if I'm still in pain that's when we'll consider having the surgery done.

Well !!! I truly was not impressed with this consultation, taken in consideration that I'm old enough and wise enough to understand, feel and except the pain on my left forearm is not something I can live with or cope with much longer unless something is done about it, now this consultation this morning with highly reputable surgeon was totally disappointing, I'm not sure if he was dealing with some of his heavy and personal issues but he showed no concern no compassion and certainly no interest at all about my left forearm, maybe I wanted some certainty, some assurance a surgery date to have something to look forward to, well that's not happening, so what will happen next is that I will go back to the drawing board and start with the Doctor to get another referral to see another surgeon to get a second opinion and then chase the insurer for another approval, sounds like fun and games, well not true, so I just need to wait and do all the chasing ever so patiently.

I guess I cannot afford to lose my cool in any way shape or form, so for me to see this surgeon this morning what took about ten minutes of consultation that was around two hundred dollars and it was totally disappointing and waste of time is really rising my anger levels, so with this surgeon there was no care factor and no compassion on how long I've been in pain and how long more will I be suffering, so as I previously mentioned before as long as this professional got paid today for ten minutes of consultation, that's all it matters.

If you ever fall in to the path of some of these professionals good luck you'll need it. Anyway as you can imagine I arrived home a bit deflated and without any delays strait on the phone trying to arrange new appointments, new referrals and new approvals again so I can get a second opinion.

I really don't know How long is all this going to take so thinking about all this is making my blood boil again, I really don't feel good about this, I feel I need to be locked up in a cell somewhere for mine and other peoples safety, I feel there's an eruption brewing in my head, heavy breathing,, heavy breathing, I need to be left alone in the back yard with my cigarettes and coffees.

I think it would be safe for me not to see or speak to anyone for the rest of the evening and night and until the early hours of the morning, and I also think this is the time where I will use a big portion of my inner strength to begin a new day tomorrow. I will pray for more patience and strength.

October 8, 2019.

I've cancelled the appointment with the psychiatrist this morning, yeah spend most of the night outside last night it was okay.

I did manage to keep the lid on things and I did managed to keep cool so therefore I do not want to see the psychiatrist this morning to rekindle any of the stuff that I've managed to keep under control, I still don't want to see anyone, for the moment I only want to concentrate on the appointments about getting my left forearm repaired, rest of the day and night I just want some peace and quiet.

October 11, 2019.
Seen the physio this afternoon and gave her the forms from the surgeon that I had useless consultation with on the seventh of this month, on those forms are some exercises for the physio to perform on my left forearm, anyhow she worked on the left shoulder for a while on some strengthening and movements, and then she started working on the left forearm.

She's done the ultra sound heat treatment on my forearm and then rubbed some cream around the sore area to the point of increasing the pain where I had to ask her to stop! And then she's trying to explain to me why it is necessary to perform these exercises on my forearm, and I tried to explain to her that I'm a bit reluctant to perform or give consent to any of these useless exercises but on the same breath.

Okay, I will abide with whatever my treaders are instigating me to go by for my physical recovery, for now I'm just hoping to find a surgeon that's not going to stuff me around and just get to the point to repair my left forearm, I keep saying time after time that I just want my forearm to be repaired so that I can get on with my life, maybe one day, who knows maybe I should start believing that miracles can happen.

Chapter
16

October 12, 2019.

After yesterdays therapy with physio the work that was done on my left forearm had a painful side effect throughout the night, last night not much sleep again and the pain killers were not helping at all, so today I felt agitated and in a very dangerous rage, every little thing was escalating the anger levels to the maximum.

I was not in a right state of mind, I yelled and screamed at my wife for no reason at all and then took her car to do something unimaginable, I wanted to end at least four peoples life's today as well as mine, oh yeah I was ready for it more ways than one, I was all geared up.

I guess the only thing stopped me today was I couldn't get these people in one area at the same time so now that I can't action the ideation I'm shaking with anger and somewhat disappointment I was lucky enough to drive in to a train station car park, even though I was very angry and almost out of it I was able to park the car in an orderly fashion, I don't know how but I did.

It took me over two hours to calm down and tried to get my head back in order, I'm finding that controlling my moods, my anger and my way of thinking is getting harder and harder, I get really scared and then I start to cry like a little boy loudly, now that I'm calm I can see that It was totally unfair the way I treated my wife before I left the house, she really did not deserve my stupid, angry and violent outburst, good thing is that I did not touch her I did not hit her, no matter how bad things get in my head I know one thing for sure that I can never ever hurt her physically, so I'm thinking when I get home I have to apologize profusely to her and hope she understands, excepts my apology and forgives me, I truly don't mean to hurt her in any way, day's like today I truly believe that I'm slipping in to a nihilistic state of mind where I can't see clearly or think clearly, now because I'm been put in this predicament by some useless people and at times when I lose it and the sparks that's protruding and flying of me hits the ones I love the most and burns them, so this does make me take the pledge that if it ever comes to a point where I have to end it all one thing is for sure is that I will take some useless people with me.

I can't talk to anyone about any of this or the ideations, I also know I shouldn't be feeling or thinking about any of this, and I certainly shouldn't be telling anyone, and maybe I shouldn't put any of it on these pages, but I'm starting to do it because this is what I feel and how I feel today, one day I'm hoping that this will be over and I'll get my life back in order that I might be able to help someone, but in saying all that I feel that there's still a lot of rocky roads ahead.

October 14, 2019.
Seen the psychologist again this morning, nothing new nothing different, we spoke for an hour about my left shoulder and my left forearm, the best advice from her was to just go along with what's happening with doctors, surgeons and physio and so on, and not much else for the rest of the day and night, back to my coffees and cigarettes and try to keep cool best I can, after the burning rage I've had last few days it sure does take a long time to bring the pressure down.

Back to my isolation where it's safe for me and everyone else, I would like to write more but It's the usual bullshit spinning around in my head.

October 17, 2019.
Just another quite day today like it has been last couple of days, up and out of bed very early this morning, not much sleep again, constant mild to severe pain on left forearm but with pain killers and sleeping pills I'm trying to get by day after day.

At times like now the only thing that makes it a bit easy is that I am excepting it is what it is, I was meant to cop this, I was meant to go through this maybe if it doesn't kill me it might make me a better person, ha ha wow there was a bit of humour there. Mmmmmm.

October 18, 2019.
Seen the physio this morning, I've told her about the treatment she applied on my left forearm last Friday that it has aggravated the pain on my left forearm so that last Friday and last Saturday the pain become somewhat unbearable.

We stopped the physio treatment on my injured left forearm, and we did have a little chat that with escalated physical pain together with my moods and my at times uncontrollable anger issues becomes too much to calm down as quickly as I would like to, so she understood and excepted that we won't apply any physio treatment on my left forearm until after the surgery, if there's going to be surgery we still don't know yet, time and patience oh by the way a jar of coffee used to last up to six to eight weeks in my household now the same size jar of coffee I can go through in less than a week.

I know too much coffee is not good for my health but I'm thinking that it could have been worst, I could have turned to alcohol or some other hard substances.

October 21, 2019.
Seen my lawyer today to organize my will, just checking in to some important things like a funeral insurance, life insurance, my superfund and my very own plot, just in case things turn sour so I don't leave financial burden on my family, how exciting.

At the same time I guess I'm looking for some valid stuff to distract myself from constant stewing in my own misery, not easy but needs to be done, I also feel the need to mention that my close friend that I've known over forty five years and his wife beautiful couple that constantly call and check up on me.

I really do appreciate it, pity the rest of my friends had walked out on me, it really doesn't seem to matter I'll get by with what I have, I do appreciate the genuinty and the loyalty of the people around me at the moment, that's enough for me.

October 23, 2019.
Meeting was organized for me to go to the city with the insurer, so I requested a taxi there and back and attended the meeting with my wife by my side, so the meeting started with my case manager and the insurers psychologist to find out where I'm at both mentally and physically, so the beginning of the meeting was good and gentle with concerning questions until that dreadful question was freely thrown at me wether I still want to harm myself ? well that hit me like a sledge hammer.

I stopped and posed for a while and then I asked my wife to leave the meeting for about five minutes, and then once again I felt compelled to explain to these two professionals the depth of the question and how intimidating and stressful answering this question can be, well for a start my wife doesn't know about my suicidal ideations and for a person to be asked constantly if they are going to harm themselves it kind of feels like an enticement are you going to do it? Are you going to do it? Are you going to do it?

Wow right now writing about this I can feel my stress levels are going higher and starting to get emotional, anyway getting back to the meeting, I reluctantly explained to them that these kind of questions should not be thrown at someone that's almost out of it, one that's on the path of suicidal ideations should not be reminded so the ideations don't have a chance to reignite with instigated questions, well they listened they've thanked me for explaining with clear consequences of what's at risk, and then one of them told me that a member of their family was on the path of suicide intentions and now this person I spoke to had a bit more understanding, even though the meeting ended well I just couldn't help walking out of the meeting with tears in my eyes knowing at one stage it got a bit emotional.

Once my wife and I left the building I just couldn't wait to get home to my confinement where I can go out in the back yard and be myself wether I want to cry or just sit there as long as it takes for my emotions to reset again, and when we did get home that's exactly what I've done until after midnight, so that's life again, it goes on and it must.

October 25, 2019.
Physio again this morning, strengthening the shoulder and getting more movements, a bit flat today, feeling tired of constantly going over and over of the same things in my head, oh boy I feel so alone and so down, the sad feeling is that I feel I have nothing left to hold on to.

I'm scared that I'm slipping through the cracks of whatever it's worth, I think I need to stop here now I can feel myself breathing heavy again and about to get emotional again.

October 27, 2019.
Not much to write about last few days, it's just the same, I've ran out of my pills I need to get some more when I see the work injury doctor on Wednesday, yeah I get sick of writing about the same old shit all the time, I write it because that's what happens day in day out.

However if I could get my left forearm repaired I would like to think that it might make a lot of difference to my mental state and it might give me some hope and confidence that everything will get back to normal again, one can only hope, one good thing out of all this is that I haven't hurt anyone severely yet or anything else.

October 28, 2019.
Seen the psychologist again this morning, when I last spoke to Miss X she wanted me to ask the psychologist some questions like is there anything I can do or practise at home and meditation and feedback on my progress, had a chat with the psychologist about the insurer, my left shoulder and my left forearm.

Even though it was fruitless again but it was okay I guess better than nothing at this stage, anyhow half way through my session she put me through a fifteen minute meditation which did not work, I find it extremely hard to relax when there's a constant pain in my left forearm and obviously my head is not in a good state, she told me to go on line when I get home and find myself a suitable meditation and to try and relax in my own environment.

On the way home in the taxi I get a call from Miss X telling me that she has changed my appointment with work injury doctor from Wednesday to Tuesday instead, well again that didn't go down to well with me but I felt I have no option to except like I do with everything else, so Miss X is back on board ever so eager to get me back to work, so what really gets to me is that her incompetent and unprofessional attitude together with her lack of people skills really heightens me to a point that it drastically slows down my mental recovery and also her disrespectfulness is another thing that each time I get a phone call, message or an email from her it's always about me going back to work.

I never get asked by Miss X on how I feel or how am I coping both mentally or physically, I guess I have to question her about this one day, but at the same time I'm trying hard not to be angry with her, at the end of the day we all have a job to do no matter how competent or incompetent we are, so back home in to my isolation again never knowing for how long.

October 29, 2019.

Appointment with work injury doctor and Miss X almost two hours of consultation, we spoke extensively about me taking excessive amounts of pills, and towards our discussion to my shock she prescribed another four lots of different pain killers and asked me to write down the time and date of each and every pill I take every day, and then we spoke about my left forearm where there was no concern and definitely no duty of care was shown.

I did receive the referral to see another surgeon for my left forearm, it felt like they've done me a huge favour and Miss X and Dr001 was not happy with the progress I was making with my psychologist so they've asked me to see a new psychologist.

Well I thought why the f#@^ would I want to start all over with someone new but I kept quiet, I thought I'll stew on it when I get home, anyway the rest of the consultation was all about getting me back to work, now here's another reason why I am so angry with some of these medical professionals is that for a start I am not ready physically still recovering from a left shoulder surgery and waiting for surgery to be done on my left forearm, and then the psychiatrist is reluctant to give me a clearance to go back to work and the psychologist totally agrees with his decision and Dr 001 and Miss X are totally aware of this so why am I constantly being pushed to go back to work while I'm being considered high risk of putting other people's lives in danger, now more to the point they know I almost done the job on myself, so yeah it makes me wander where's the professionalism and where's the duty of care if not for me at least for others.

When I did get home it's quite obvious that the inevitable does happen, all of this reignites in my head where it's ready to explode and again I go deep into angry, useless and at times dangerous thoughts trying to deal with it until the early hours of the morning again, some of thoughts are who put me here and why? And I am so pissed off that Dr 001 and Miss X are doing nothing but pushing me to go back to work.

If it ever comes to a point where I will pull the plug I will not go alone, than I would rest easily when my wife and my children bring Dr 001 Miss X to justice and make sure they do some hard time to learn their lessons, ohhhh maybe I will cool off a bit later but this is what I'm feeling right now and strongly hoping that I don't put any of it into action, now I'm still wandering why did Dr 001 and Miss X totally want to ignore the recommendations from the psychiatrist and the psychologist not to send me back to work and yet I'm still being pushed wether I'm ready or not.

This only makes me understand one thing that I am just another case, just another number, they truly don't care or give a rats about me or anyone else but themselves.

Well there's a good chance all this is going to be going around and around in my head for I don't know how long.

November 1, 2019.

Physio again this morning nothing new nothing different, just another consultation and just another step closer to my recovery, still heightened from Wednesday I'm not in the mood to write anymore today.

November 2, 2019.
After Wednesdays outburst it takes me a little longer to calm down these days, I didn't want to write down all those things but that's how I felt at those moments just couldn't help myself, and with all these pain killers and the antidepressants that I'm taking by recommendations of the medical professionals it really gets very hard to explain how I feel.

I'm almost convinced that the antidepressants are making me feel like a zombie and combined with all different pain killers well, it does have a tsunami effect of mixed emotions go through my head quite often, and these feelings truly leaves me with no care factor, and sometimes I have this insatiable hunger and desire for a dangerous and a violent revenge where it gets extremely difficult to control my moods and my emotions.

I am seriously hoping that my left forearm will be repaired soon before I do something drastic, I feel the need to stop writing now, I don't know what else to write about, I don't know what to think about, I don't know what to do, I just feel lost and powerless again, no confidence, terrible feelings that lasts three to four days to ease off a little and for some stupid reason they are all back again, I'm feeling very very tired of all this, I just want it all to end, I really don't want to feel like this anymore.

November 4, 2019.
No interest in anything again today, just feeling like a zombie still with excessive pills that I'm taking, It's been drummed into my head by the useless medical professionals that I have no other option, the only hope I have now is that I have an appointment to see another surgeon for my left forearm to get a second opinion or even better he might perform the surgery on my left forearm

The appointment is on the thirteenth of this month so something to look forward to until then I'll keep on relying on these useless pain killers and antidepressants, I guess at some point I need to give some credit to these medical professionals who are treating me, I try and tell them about my pain in my forearm and I get this cold reception of disbelief, it's a feeling that if they don't see my pain.

It's not there it does not exist so the easiest thing to do is issue me with more pain killers, how appropriate, anyhow last night at a long length I kept thinking about the people who put me here and the ones who deserted me when I thought I needed them, than I find myself brewing this Antarctic storm this resentfulness towards them and relentlessly going over and over it, and then I get more angry with myself for thinking about all this, once again I find myself in a no win situation, just keep on pushing shit uphill.

November 7, 2019.

It was organized for me to attend work today for three hours on light duties by Miss X and Dr 001 but instead of three hours I could only manage two hours the reason for that was, the task that was given to me involved my fingers flicking through some large quantities of paper work where it was increasing the pain on my injured left forearm and my stomach wasn't right due to excessive pain killers that I've been taken.

My mental state didn't help much at all still on antidepressants so after a brief discussion with the OHS manager and the distribution manager I left my workplace on good terms, when I arrived home I called Dr 001 and the insurer about what had happened, they both told me not to worry and that at least I've made the effort to give it a try, so I will give it another try next week, see what happens, and the rest of the day and night is as usual same old.

November 8 2019.

Physio again today and what can I say same old treatment trying to recover as soon as I can, and my main focus today is how I still have a lot of resentment towards my work colleagues and managers at my workplace simply because of the ostracizing I've been presented by them all that is totally unacceptable and with a strong term it is absolutely unforgivable.

I am trying to come to terms with it, I am trying to except that it is what it is but it is definitely hard to do, there's not much I can do about it except well let's not go there again, not now not today, I seem to be getting used to the idea of stewing in my own misery silently on my own.

November 11, 2019.
Just because I don't mention sleepless nights, painful nights and miserable nights for quite some time doesn't mean that it's all gone away, I just don't want to talk about it constantly to the point where it gets very annoying.

Anyway, I've seen the psychologist again this morning and for some reason she has shown me some good signs of understanding me, it was a good session for a change, oh by the way Miss X wanted me to get a progress report from the psychologist and when I mentioned this to the psychologist she told me that Miss X needs to formally request a progress report herself and I mentioned this to Miss X she then referred me to the insurer for me to ask the insurer to get a progress report for Miss X.

Now my question is that if I am to do these tasks for Miss X then why is she been appointed to be the liaison person between me and all my treaders, anyway the abrupt attitude and the commanding ways of asking me to do things for her really puts her on thin ice that I do my absolute best not to lose it with her, at the same time I do my best to comply with every instruction from every direction to the best of my ability so at the end of all this with a lot of hoping and praying that with a great possibility I might have a smooth transition back to my normal and happy life again.

Well one would always try to be optimistic I guess, whether or not it works is another story.

November 13, 2019.
I don't want to talk about pills, sleepless nights or my moods and how I've been feeling it really doesn't matter and it really is very hard to find someone that can truly understand, anyhow after a long arm wrestle and what felt like an unwinnable battle to get an

approval from the insurer to see a surgeon for a second opinion and a possible date for a surgery on my left forearm is today.

After looking at the MRI scans and x-rays the surgeon told me that I definitely need the surgery done on my left forearm and gave me a surgery date at fifth of December providing I get another approval for the surgery from the insurer, here I go mixed feelings again, happy with the surgery date but dreading the idea of getting an approval on time for the surgery, hopefully I will receive the approval on time.

Anyway on the other hand it was a relief that this second surgeon seen the MRI scans and the X-rays and understood the urgency of surgically repairing my injured left forearm, wow it truly was a moment of triumph that someone actually believed me that I am in pain, this is a good feeling because sometimes people have a way of thinking that you're faking it all, well I guess no one gets surgery done on any parts of their body just to prove a point, anyway hopefully it all goes well and after the surgery on my left forearm even though it will add extra mileage to my recovery process that's combined with my left shoulder I know that it will all be worth it in the end.

I'm just trying to learn to see the bigger picture, spoke to a lady from the insurer this afternoon and explained the importance of the approval for my upcoming surgery in December and she became a bit concerned about my mixed emotions, I don't know if she has any authority to push for my approval, I'll just have to wait and see, and then I spoke with Miss X and informed her about the outcome of the consultation with the orthopaedic surgeon, but I don't think she was overly happy about that simply because she won't be able to push me to go back to work so soon, once again no concern what so ever from Miss X in fact she sounded like she was somewhat disappointed that there's a very good chance that my injured left forearm will be repaired.

Well it is very hard to get used to someone like Miss X's negative and disrespectful attitude, well then again I should be used to it because no one else gives a rats arse except my lovely wife, and everyone else is somewhat a professional in giving a great lip service, yeah well talking about mixed feelings and mixed emotions that's how it is, it's almost like when you spend enough time in the sewer you get to know the rats.

November 14, 2019.
Yeah after yesterdays mixed emotions and everything else I went to work today knowing that I wasn't going to stay the full three hours on light duties, I wanted go in and explain to the managers face to face that today I just don't have the ability to concentrate on anything at all, even though they were part of the group that helped dig my grave and pushed me in to bury me alive I still wanted to show them that I have morals, respect, personal and dignified principals that are unmatched by anyone in that place.

Then again the era we're living in there aren't many people left with these qualities, anyhow once I arrived home I called the insurer and explained about why I didn't perform my three hours of light duties this morning and then I was told to contact Dr 001 to obtain a non capacity form for this morning, once I received the form to forward it to insurer and my employer, so more clerical work for someone who is not in a right state of mind, but here's the catch if I don't perform these clerical tasks I simply don't get paid for the day, that was made very clear to me by the insurer, my employer and Miss X, once again when you're down it gets made very clear that you're not important.

November 15, 2019.
Seen the physio again this morning about my left shoulder exercises and recovery process, as well as everything is going well with the treatment from the physio I can't help having this negative feeling that the usage of my left shoulder and my left arm will ever be the same again.

At the moment I think we're about twenty five to thirty percent there, one can only hope that one day mysteriously things will get back to normal, not only on the physical side of things but mentally too, the reason of me mentioning this is that the question I get asked by medical professionals and most recently by the lady from the insurer quite freely is that do I still have suicidal ideations, even though I've made it clear to all that it's a wrong and bad question.

I hate it and then it makes my mind wandering off again, are they asking that question out of concern or are they asking it to keep their paper work in order because that's what the standard operating procedures are dictating them to do, so it's quite clear that there's no concern and definitely no duty of care, just the standard operating procedures to protect the medical professionals, in so many cases once the antidepressants are prescribed there's no follow up.

This is not an opinion and it is not an assumption I have spoken to some people who have survived the suicidal ideations and I also have spoken to some people who have lost loved ones, and one of the most important point we all had in common was that actioning the suicidal ideation is only a deep, dark and a very frightening moment away, if and when the person is ready to action it there's nothing anyone can do to stop them, if there's one advise I can give to those medical professionals is that either stop asking that dreadful question or find a new way of asking that question, the alarming concern about this question is it's not only aggravating but it can also be activating, and one other thing, when a person is heightened to a very dangerous levels of pursuing or actioning the suicidal ideations at that point hearing that kind of questions can be deleterious.

November 17, 2019.

Got out of bed very early this morning, feeling a bit more flat than usual, more questions in my head, more doubt in my head and I feel as if I am sinking deeper, I don't know why.

I don't know how I just don't understand, maybe it has a lot to do with the way I felt yesterday, I know one thing for sure it's a long way down, it's too deep, it's too dark and it's too lonely, I'm finding out that I've got nobody except my wife, my son and the two good friends that we've known over forty years, even though we might not see each other as often as we would like to but they constantly call and check on how am I coping and if there's anything I need, and the rest of the friends together with some family members have become nothing but acquaintances, they've become people where we just say hello to each other from a distance.

It's sad so sad but not much I can do about it, sometimes I think that my involuntary isolation is not helping with my social life but then again judging by the way how some people had walked out on me is not comforting at all, when you're alone you truly are alone, anyhow I'm getting very tired of all this, very tired of constant negative, bad, sad and at times dangerous thoughts.

I need a break from all this, it really hurts my head and here I go again difficulty breathing and my eyes are watering ready to go in the back yard in a secluded area where I can cry like a little boy again, just can't help it that's how life is at the moment.

November 18, 2019.

Seen the WI-DR [work injury Doctor] this morning, she's given me the same amount of pain killers, sleeping pills and antidepressants wow how lucky am I and she gave me a non capacity form until the tenth of December that's if the surgery on my left forearm doesn't go ahead, but if the surgery does go ahead on the fifth of December WI-DR won't see me for quite some time well she's done her job.

When I arrived home I've emailed the non capacity forms to my employer, the insurer and Miss X and no reply, I wander why I guess that's another story, however a lot of these issues are adding up more and more on my plate to deal with day in day out, on the contrary though I should be thankful that I still have the good old spiritual strength, mental strength and being able to differentiate between right and wrong.

I know there are a lot of times I feel weak, I think I'm losing it but for whatever the reason is I seem to be holding it together, anyhow I don't want to mention anything about last night, how I cried like a little boy, heavy pain on my left forearm medium pain on my left shoulder and the issues in my head which feels like a ton of bricks no I don't want to talk about it, I know with me constantly talking about it keeps it all alive like an ever burning flames where the heat can get quite unbearable.

November 19, 2019.

I've seen the psychiatrist this afternoon, he wrote a few things down on his laptop and then he asked me some questions which had no worthiness to my condition what so ever, I showed him the prescription I've received the day before from the WI-DR.

He looked at it smiled and said keep taking these and we'll hope for the best and that was it, such a short consultation and so expensive, four hundred dollars for fifteen minutes, and he is so busy that he won't be able to see me until next year in fact the eleventh of February, wow and wow I just don't know and I don't understand what he does and what kind of a report he gives to the rest of the medical professionals not that I care or give a rats arse but as I mentioned before some of these people are full of shit, they only speculate and assume to know or understand your mental state, no direct knowledge and they get away with it and make shit loads of money.

Anyway it is hard for me to except that I'm seeing a psychiatrist simply because of my upbringing, until the age of fourteen before I arrived in to this country it was imperative for us to except that man don't cry, man don't show emotions and man definitely don't see a psychiatrist if you do see a psychiatrist you're an idiot and you're stupid, even though I've been in this country for so many years and yet these kinds of undignified and powerfully dictated policies that were imprinted in my head, and at times it is extremely hard to shake off, that's one of the reasons why I seem to struggle with a lot of issues, but then again in all fairness where I came from in those years that's the only way they knew how to build a young boy in to becoming a man a strong man at that, and yeah today I would like to think that I am spiritually, mentally and in my heart a very strong person.

The way I feel right now is that I let myself down, yeah speaking about down as the days go by I'm finding myself slipping further down day by day, I'm feeling weak in ways that I've never imagined before, and I'm finding myself frighteningly and completely out of love for anyone and anything and I feel too weak, too uninterested and I feel too sad, too down and too lonely to except love, yeah it's a true discovery that you get to know your true family and friends, no one understands, no one takes the time to truly understand, so apart from the physical pain which sometimes hard to hide but your mental pain well you learn to live with it and to the best of your ability you learn to hide it, one of the reasons for that is you really don't want to hurt the one's that truly loves you.

November 22, 2019.
Physio again this morning, nothing new, nothing different, slow process is starting to get to me, and I can feel that my circadian rhythm is being disrupted, not controllable, not tolerable, feels like I'm in the middle of the ocean in the rough seas where there are no life savers in sight, sink or swim from here on so good luck.

    I don't feel like thinking or writing today or next few days, I just want to dim down that ever burning miserable flame or better still I want to put it out permanently, I hope I can find some optimism that in the very near future this will be all over and done with, what a relief that would be, yeah I truly don't want to talk about last night and what misery I might be going through next few days.

    I guess what I'm trying to say is that I just want to have the feeling of being neutral completely, not to think about anything, not to worry about anything and most importantly not to cry about anything at all, I truly miss that feeling, I hope I'll get it back again one day, however I'm not a quitter but when you're down and just about out you seem to have no strength left to fight anything anymore, just got to keep breathing and keep pushing through.

Chapter 17

November 25, 2019.
Seen the psychologist again this morning, I've expressed how I'm feeling about not hearing from the insurer regarding the approval of my left forearm surgery, I know I was a bit too heavy on the deliverance of how I felt.

I told her that this could be the very last consultation with her and that I'm done, I told her that I don't know where to go what to do how to act or how to react to anything anymore, this is true I didn't know if I was going to get home today, for all this the psychologist showed me some concern and assured me that she will contact the insurer and asked me to calm down and not to do anything irrational and to go straight home and be safe, and I did just that I went home, and tried to change the stormy whirlpool effect in my head, starting to think about my recent behaviour, especially with our good friends dropped in yesterday, apparently my behaviour was bad and not acceptable.

I've seen that in my wife's face and in her voice and of course this makes me sad and more angry knowing that this is not me, where the hell is this unreasonable behaviour is coming from, by now it's mid afternoon while I'm thinking about all this I've received a phone call from the insurer that I have the approval for my left forearm surgery to go ahead on the fifth of December.

Well I sat down for at least an hour motionless with tears rolling down my face, I didn't know what I was feeling, was I happy, was I excited, was I angry or was I relieved that it was going to finally go ahead with getting my left forearm repaired so in time I can get my life back in order, I'm not sure what input my psychologist had with the insurer but hey it worked and I've got my approval, anyway the rest of the day and night I will profusely apologise to my wife for my unreasonable and unacceptable behaviour in order to maintain and continue the undying love and respect I have for my wife, as I keep mentioning that she doesn't deserve any of this, I would like to make her see and believe that this is my battle and one day I will definitely overcome all this, this is my pledge I hope I can carry it through to end this misery once and for all.

November 26, 2019.
Well again I don't want to talk about how my night was and how I got out of bed early hours of the morning and had excessive amounts of coffees and cigarettes again, not only it gets me more miserable more annoying but boring as well, instead I want to try and be a little bit positive about the news of me receiving the approval of my left forearm surgery on the fifth of December.

I want to try hard today to lift my spirits a little higher if I can, I have already apologized to my wife and today I will apologize to my son and our close friends of forty five years about my recent behaviours and outbursts, I hope it won't be too hard to be forgiven by the people I love and respect.

I am in the optimistic hope that my unreasonable behaviour recently is not me it's not in my character, I will sit in here in my miserable environment waiting patiently to be forgiven and at the same time keep looking forward to getting my left forearm surgery done and get the recovery process over and done with as soon as possible so I can start seeing some light at the end of my tunnel.

It is ironic that I've never believed in hope before but now I am finding myself to be very hopeful in certain areas of my life, I guess the reason for not believing in hope relates to my upbringing is that you are strong and you have common sense so you don't heavily rely or depend on hope you simply take matters in to your own hands and deal with it as best as you can, and if you couldn't you were weak and useless, that was the environment I grew up in until the age of fourteen.

November 27, 2019.
Appointment with the second orthopaedic surgeon this afternoon to confirm the date the fifth of December and finalize some details in preparation for my left forearm surgery, so yeah I am relieved a bit, I waited almost seven years for this especially in the last eight months it really was very difficult to make people understand and except that I was constantly in pain, the only thing on offer was the pain killers all this time, it might be unbelievable and unacceptable but this is the reality.

I'm sure I'm not the only one this happens to, but maybe I'm one of very few that remembers these important issues and have the courage and ability to highlight them, now finally something is getting done about my injured left forearm I guess it's better late than never, good way to look at it, well after the surgery in completion of the recovery and getting all the necessary clearances resume my employment until where I can gracefully retire but whether or not this optimistic assumption of mine becoming a reality could be another story.

Out of all the negative and at times dangerous thoughts that goes through my mind sometimes I don't know how but I can find a little glimpse of hope that maybe some positive things may happen in the near future, so therefore I do optimistically entertain some unrealistic and unsupportive thoughts in my head and this could be five percent of the twenty four hour cycle, and the rest of the ninety-five percent at the moment same old same old the usual misery.

December 2, 2019.
I haven't been writing anything in the last few days, I just don't seem to have any focus on anything at the moment, I'm extremely worried about my wife, we don't see eye to eye and our conversations are very short and at times are cold.

With what I'm going through at the moment I can truly understand my wife that she is not a medical professional and has no knowledge on how to handle me or how to treat me I'm saying this with no disrespect so therefore I can see her getting frustrated with me I can see her hurting, we have been together for forty five years so this is all new to both of us and yes we're both getting frustrated, sad and angry that we're not like we used to be.

Once this is all over I will make it up to my wife I will do my best to bring our love alive again, I love her and I want to show her, we both know how strain full it has been on our love and marriage in the last eight months, with all these hurtful feelings in my head and in my heart and the hurt I've caused my wife certainly dictates me to hold certain people accountable, oh yeah I do want to be responsible for these certain people to take their last breath in my presence but that's another issue I won't pay any more attention to for the moment.

Once again I know I shouldn't be writing things like these but I want to be true and honest about what I write and this is what and how I feel right now, tomorrow or the next day might be a different feelings and different situation altogether, maybe there will come a day where I will be able to control my thoughts and my feelings, one will never know.

Chapter 18

December 5, 2019.
Yes!!!!! It's the surgery day finally here today at a private hospital in east of Melbourne, so I arrived at the hospital at ten thirty this morning filled in some forms and started to wait to be called in, sat and waited till six pm and then they took me in to prepare me for the surgery.

About seven thirty I was taken into the operating room, after the surgery about ten pm they took me into the recovery room, obviously with the anaesthetics and pain killers I was out of it until two am, woke up with nurses checking on me and giving me more pain killers and then trying to go to sleep.

December 6, 2019.
Couldn't get much sleep with the nurses checking up on me constantly and given me more pain killers throughout the night, now it's eight am had two more pain killers.

After the surgeon, the pharmacist and the physio signing the release forms went down stairs and called a cab, I had taxi codes given to me by the insurer, I had arrived here yesterday no problem but this morning she is telling me that today's code had expired, with me having the surgery less than twenty four hours I felt my patience were running very thin and I needed a taxi urgently so I half exploded and told the lady from the taxi department that I don't give a rats arse about the cost and just get me a f#$%ing taxi and she did with no compassion and no concern to what I just told her about me having the surgery done.

Anyhow when I arrived home the very first thing was to have my coffees and cigarettes firstly to calm down and then start to think about the new journey to another physical recovery and continue to battle and try to overcome my mental instability, getting home with all the pain killers that had been pumped in to my system kept me pain free until about 8pm than the pain killers started to wear off so not long after that I took one of the pills I received from the hospital.

The pill was five hundred milligram, yeah powerful but not enough to give me any comfort but somehow I managed throughout the night, anyhow while I'm trying to cope with the physical side of my new journey to recovery for some reason I can't seem to control the speed in my head at the moment, it's going too fast things are popping up in my head faster than I can give each issue enough time to deal with one at the time, so up goes the stress levels again and not to mention the anger.

I guess once again I'm getting frustrated thinking of things like how long is this recovery journey going to take this time?, how long am I going to deal with my mental state? How soon will I get back to my employment?, am I ever going to get the full usage of my left shoulder and arm again?

Is my wife and I ever going to be on the same page again? If the pain killers and the sleeping pills were supposed to knock me out for the night it's not working, simply because me trying to deal with all these issues in my head almost immediately is overpowering the effects of the pills, I have spoken about me tapping into my inner strength and using my inner powers to deal with all these, and sometimes this worries me thinking how much inner strength do I have left? And when will it run out? And if I do run out my inner strength does that mean this will be the end?

Right now I know it might be wrong for me to have excessive amounts of coffees and cigarettes but unfortunately they are the only tools I have to see the night through, and hopefully tomorrow will be a different day a better day, one can only hope.

December 7, 2019.
Here I go again, up and early out of bed still very dark outside, with a bit of difficulty managed to make myself a coffee grabbed my cigarettes and went outside, and then looked at the time it's only one forty am so I have a long day ahead I thought to myself.

Well one good thing is that I have stocked up on my coffee and cigarettes so I can face the long days ahead without annoying anyone at all, as I'm sitting here trying to welcome a brand new day a new sunrise maybe a new beginning I'm experiencing a heavy almost unbearable pain on my left arm running all the way down to my finger tips, the excruciating pain between one and ten is about nine, so it's three am now I took two of the pain killers I received from the hospital.

I just need to sit here wait patiently until the next lot of pills and the antidepressants, no other choice, I just need to ride it through, I truly wish that it was only the physical recovery that I had to go through without all the other issues on my mind it would have been so much easier so that I could devote all my attention on just one thing, there's this certain warm gladness arises from within and in my head that I have this opportunity and the ability to be able to write all my daily thoughts and activities on a daily basis and hopefully if I make it to the finish line and come out of this battle of mine alive is that there's is a good chance I might be able to help some people who might think that there's no way out of all this.

It's a long lonely journey with so many hills to climb but at the moment I'm in too much pain physically and mentally to be able to put a finger on the exact point or the points on what helps me to keep a lid on some dangerous and at times risky ideations, but I hope soon to find the reasons to why am I not letting go, sometimes I also wish that we had the ability to open the tops of our heads and grab all the issues and put it all in to a cardboard box close the lids and put a sticky tape on it until we're ready to reopen it again and pull out an issue one at a time to deal with it pleasantly in our own peaceful environment, yeah wouldn't that be good?

I guess not many of us had discovered that ability or the possibility yet, anyway it's ten am now painful left arm and I can't move my left fingers at all so I took another two oxycodone pain killers, so throughout the day and night it was a bit of a Marching thing that was happening between the lounge room and the outside, because smoking in the house is forbidden.

December 8, 2019.

Day three after the surgery on my left forearm, as a result of the continuous consumption of pain killers throughout the night has decreased the pain to a moderate level for the moment, so this allowed me to have a shave, shower and breakfast with the help from my wife by ten am this morning, wow another triumphant moment.

If my left arm wasn't bandaged I think I would have high fived myself, anyhow lack of sleep last night and the pain starting to increase again so I took two of paracetamol pain killers and laid on the couch in the lounge room until mid afternoon, still feeling effects of agoraphobia and still isolating quite heavily, just can't help myself, still continuing with the antidepressants together with all the pain killers, That's life, must go on.

December 9, 2019.

Even though I'm in pain and suffering both physically and mentally but for some reason I don't know where it came from or what instigated it but there's a little bit of an optimism in the air, I seem to want to spend and stay on the five percent of the positive side of my day rather than the ninety-five percent of my miserable side of my twenty four hour day, I don't know how long it will last but I want to stay connected to this feeling for as long as it take.

I guess I have the time in my recovery process so I don't have to rush, anyway I've cancelled two of my appointments this morning one of them was the first surgeon who operated on my left shoulder I will call back and make another appointment at a later date, and the second one was with the WI-Dr.

Having received a non capacity form until the early January from the second surgeon who operated on my left forearm so therefore I didn't feel the need to see the WI-Dr, the only point of her seeing me is that she'll make extra earnings no other reason at this point, and yes I had the approval of the insurer about the cancellations of these two appointments, as I have mentioned it before that I'm trying to do everything right by every medical professional so there's no confusion at all, anyway the thought of going through another marathon recovery process with the physio and every other medical professional can be a bit daunting but the good thing at the moment is that I'm on the path of recovery even though it's slow but my attitude is becoming a little bit more positive than the first surgery I've had June this year on my left shoulder.

In saying all this I would like to mention one thing again, throughout this ordeal in the last eight months I've come to see and understand the originality and unoriginality of the people I've been associating with all these years, the true family members and the true friends that I can count and the number would be very low, my wife number one, she has been through a lot with me, I haven't been easy, especially when I hit rock bottom not that I'm out of the woods yet but the more I think the more I can see how unreasonable I have been.

I owe my wife so much and then there's my son, he's been fantastic, genuine, concerned, loving and understanding and most importantly sitting down with me and listening to what I had to say without any interruption and without judgement, how good is that, and my dearest friends that I've known over forty years that have been there for me caring, listening and guiding me in my hour of darkness too many times and then there's my brother constantly calling to check up on me to see how I'm travelling and if there's anything he can do for me, so yes I am surrounded by some good and genuine people that are making it easier for me to resist the temptation of actioning the ideation of pulling the plug and ending it all at once.

Out of all this what I am trying to say is that when you're down and just about out and you're spending so much time alone is when you realize who is fake and who is real, and I guess the real ones are the ones who shine a light on your path to help you get out of the darkness, if you are willing and somewhat strong enough to walk on the path that has been lit up for you, well it's up to you which direction you want to take in the darkest hour of your life.

One thing for sure is that at the end of the day no matter what anyone says or does it is up to each individuals prerogative on what path one wants to walk on, every now and then I seem to get a glimpse of hope a tiny bit of light at the end of my tunnel that has a good chance of lifting my spirits up a little bit but then one negative conversation with one of the medical professionals or the insurer can push me down to the bottom again, so quite often it becomes a battle that's not worth fighting for.

December 11, 2019.

After another uncomfortable night last night without going too much into it I've asked my wife to take me to my mum's, it was great to see mum, I have so much love and respect for my mum and get the same in return, so the conversations we get in to have no boundaries and no judgement it is so natural it lifts my spirits up a little bit until I get home trying to resist not to enter into the prison of misery and not to jump onto the treadmill of self destruction again and again.

It does take a lot of mental energy and a lot of inner strength to try and stay focused, anyway about three pm this afternoon the pain on my left arm became unbearable so around four pm I took one tablet that was seven hundred and fifty milligram slow release that I received from the hospital, this thing was so powerful that within the hour I could hardly stand on my feet, I think I was meant to take this pill before bed time, oh well we live and learn I guess.

After the surgery on my left arm last Thursday it almost feels like a mini miracle that every now and then I seem to have the ability to look and analyse things from different angles but unfortunately there are still no answers to a lot of my questions as to what's been happening in the last eight months, what I'm still going through and how long more will I go through all this.

I still find it hard to except some peoples perspectives of where I am at the moment, one of the main reasons is why I isolate myself to the point of being agoraphobic, I find some peoples false kindness and fake understanding can be patronizing and intimidating I'm just not in the mood for any sweet whispers into my ears. The way I feel right now I really don't care if these pages become published one day is that I need to openly and honestly mention two of the most loyal people in my life that's helping me unconditionally and lovingly are my wife and my son, their dedication and devotion makes me become teary quite often, they are one of the reasons why I am still here.

December 12, 2019.
Just another usual night, limited amount of time in bed and limited sleep, every time I move my left arm slightly the pain increases to a level where I need to take more pain killers, the irony of this is that the pain increases immediately and it takes forever to reduce it to a comfortable level, spending so much time at home in the recovery process it is inevitable that I do a lot of thinking.

Here's another admission since the beginning of this ordeal is that I have conversations with myself, I talk to myself especially early hours of the morning in the back yard in the dark, before my ordeal started over eight months ago I used to think that people who talk to themselves are idiots but hey I think differently now, I'm thinking now when I talk to people they are hearing me but they're not listening, they try and show some concern without understanding and in most cases there's no one available to talk to, so this leaves the field openly available for me to have conversations with myself, and now I sheepishly think that there's nothing wrong with that.

I guess I'm not hurting anyone, now on the more positive side I am trying to push myself to gain some confidence and try to see things a bit more clearer.

I know and except that there are lots and lots of baby steps ahead, but the down side of this is when I feel that I've been disrespected or disregarded for whatever the reason is when the positivity and the possibility of raising above all becomes a huge hurdle, that's when I find myself spiralling down towards the bottom again and I also know the prevention to all this is that I shouldn't be taking notice of people's opinions or sweet whispers but it is human nature I just can't seem to help it and I can't help myself getting caught up in peoples whirlpool of gossiping assumptions, some of these people I'm talking about are very close to me so I thought and some are immediate family members that I lost and they've lost me, it is what it is I just need to concentrate on moving forward I guess.

December 13, 2019.

Another brand new day beginning, just like I've done so many in fact countless mornings around two, three am I'm outside downing coffees and unlimited cigarettes and watching the night become day.

So peaceful, as usual this allows me to do a lot of thinking, with my left arm being bandaged from my wrist all the way up past my elbow and the thought of marathon recovery process is once again increasing the stress levels, with limited movement on the left arm and shoulder, equals to limited activities simple things like toilet, showering, shaving, brushing teeth, getting dressed and shoe laces, each time I action any of these activities so many colourful words with anger comes out of my mouth, so it is understandable the added anger on top of what I'm already dealing mentally can become uncontrollable at times to a point where everything becomes negative and whatever I think of has no worthiness at all, and when all this activates in my head it almost happens so suddenly but to calm down and get out of this can take days

Another regrettable thing about this is that it constantly takes me back to the nineteenth of April and the twelfth of October this year where I've almost actioned the unthinkable so it's quite obvious that the pilot light to disastrous action or actions will be burning for a very long time, at the moment as I'm thinking and writing about all this is giving me goose bumps and makes me become teary again.

Sometime in the near future I need to get out of this completely, right now I'm struggling with hope not having future not having trust in anyone and not being able to count or rely on anyone, the reason I'm feeling like this is that I've hit bottom.

It's too deep it's too dark and it's too f*&^ing lonely, here I go I'm getting more angry again.

December 16, 2019.

I've cancelled my psychologist appointment this morning and had an argument with the person who was doing the cancelling.

I told her to get off the phone in not so good terms, simply because she wanted me to pay cancellation fee, she was persistent so my good nature took a bad turn, sometimes I find it appropriate to cancel some of these sessions so that I'm not constantly reminded of anything from the last nine months, I would like to think that I'm trying to do my best to get out of the darkness, I feel tired I feel worn out, I feel that I have very little strength left, without these sessions I do enough to remind myself of my darkness and my almost down and out times, so I do want to leave it all behind and with great apologies to my wife and my son it would be great to start living a normal life again.

Hey I'm trying, and again I did not write anything last couple of days, I still go through blank hours and days where I have no desire for anything, I simply prefer to go to my usual spot in the backyard and stay in silence, sometimes it's the best medicine for me for more ways than one, I don't hurt anyone and I don't get hurt or angry for useless situations and with useless f^*&ing people, oh I tried to do meditation online today with the duration of thirty-five minutes I think I only lasted about five minutes, not ready yet.

December 22, 2019.

Oh boy here I go again I had no interest in writing about anything the last five days, still sitting in the backyard a lot, staring into the emptiness and constantly thinking, thinking about a lot of things that maybe all be nonsense but just can't help myself

Yesterday afternoon couple of friends came to visit and have a coffee with us, it felt like a hospital visit they kept looking at their watches they couldn't wait to leave I couldn't help wandering did they come to see me out of concern or did they came to find out if my situation was real or fake so they can have something to gossip about, again I can't help thinking like this, I guess this just gave me another reason why I shouldn't associate with fake people.

The way I feel right now I truly mean that, anyway it's my son's birthday today and we were meant to go to a restaurant last night or maybe tonight well I've declined with apology to my son that I'm just not ready to mingle with so many people at the same time

He wasn't happy about it but he showed me some kindness and excepted my apology, I except everyone has their own issues and one of my main issue at the moment is that I'm sick of faking my smile, I'm sick of telling my wife that everything is okay, I'm sick of acting that I'm okay.

I did not write anything the last few days again it's that I'm finding it very hard to get off the bottom, I can't express and I can't explain the feeling of being down, this shit is f%^&ing real no one understands, people say they do but little do they know is that they have no f%^&ing idea, I just don't want to speak to people who's knowledge is purely based on assumptions or what they've read in books or the useless information they've obtained from social media, I know there are people out there who are going through a similar situation as me but hey how the hell do you find the genuine ones.

I have yet to find someone that can sit with me without being intimidating patronizing to have an open and honest conversation with me, oh well again it is what is just keep on paddling against the currant.

December 23, 2019.

Yeah just another day just another beginning where it could have been so good so productive full of happiness full of loving and respectful people around and then I open my eyes and get in touch with reality and I can't tell you how disappointing that is, just to find out how unrealistic, cunning, knaving and back stabbing some people have became.

How the genuinity of some people have faded away, I'm thinking like this because it's true, maybe because I'm from the old school, the old fashion qualities of love and respect I guess maybe this is one of the reasons why I find it so hard to comprehend and except where I am right now, I know I seem to be writing about the same things over and over again.

I don't mean it I guess these are the things constantly goes around and around in my head and I live with all this on daily basis, It is extremely hard to find someone that can sit with you, talk to you and listen to you, oh some people do sit with you and listen to you if you pay them handsomely, well that's another story, here I am writing all this, well in my recovery process I do have all day and all night, writing this page alone can take up to four hours, as I'm writing I start thinking of some of the unthinkable and my mind wanders off, just like it is happening now and by the end of it I end up in one of two pointless path's, one of them is full of emptiness with lots of blanks and unanswered questions and the other is full of rage, fright and head full of dangerous thoughts.

I'm still trying to be optimistically hopeful, but for now back to my usual tools of coffees and cigarettes in the back yard with my miserable thoughts and tears not knowing how long do I have to go through with all this.

December 24, 2019.

Came in the house after midnight, spend a bit of time outside again, about five am this morning walking out in to the backyard through a sliding door I knocked my left forearm that's in a sling against the door jam and the pain obviously escalated all the way to ten plus out of ten so the language came out of my mouth was very colourful and it had some volume that some of the neighbours lights came on where I was compelled to apologize and calm down.

It was no fault of theirs and I have no problem with any of them, so back to the thinking process again with my coffee and cigarettes, thinking a lot is what I do lots of now, I'm finding that there are lots of questions being created in my head, two of the main ones are who created this misery in my life in the last eight to nine months and why? Because I have so much time now so therefore I pay so much attention to these questions and each time I try my hardest to find suitable answers each time I fail, so again the inevitable happens,

I'm angry yeah I'm angry with the whole situation and this anger becomes fuelled even more when I think about the people who instigated this misery and put me in to this hole.

I cannot except and I cannot forgive and I don't want to hide it anymore and yes I did entertain the thought of pulling the trigger at couple of occasions and take satisfying revenge, but the family, the family, the family I don't know if my family are my strength or my weakness but the thought of them makes me question the dangerous thoughts in my head.

I'm not convinced or certain yet that they are the sole reason as to why I don't action any ideations, one think I'm sure of is that it would be totally unfair for them to visit me in jail or six foot under for my moment of madness in order to eventuate a totally useless and maybe invalidated revenge, but never the less it is human nature to contemplate some of the unthinkable and even in some cases unimaginable and frightening actions, however some days I do go through the day without any consideration on any of the circumstances that I might hurt or let my family down where it gets me scared to the point of me trembling in my skin.

Hey, some days I don't think of any of the above doesn't mean that I'm over it or it's all gone and forgotten, no, what constantly remains lit and alive is the pilot light, knowing that and the feel of that never goes away, it actually gets scary at times that it might ignite without warning, I'm trying with all my might to keep the lid on it firmly, it gets tiring very tiring not only mentally but physically as well, however I am confident for some reason that one day I will find someone I can talk to about all this that will understand me, one can be hopeful at times, but no resolution yet.

Chapter 19

December 25, 2019.
My first dark Christmas ever with physical pain and mental instability with heavily developed agoraphobia, I can feel it's not going to be a good day, I don't want to write anymore today, I just can't hide or stop my tears .

December 27, 2109.
Last couple of days no emotions at all completely numb and blank to everything and everyone, today there are a couple of pockets or spurs in my day that allows me to get back to my usual thinking again and then blank again for the most of the day, it's almost midnight I'm writing this even though I've had lots of coffees and cigarettes throughout the day and night.

I don't know how much more coffees and cigarettes I will have and how long am I going to stay awake for so I'll keep writing down what I feel, yeah xmas just past a couple of days ago even though I personally don't celebrate xmas but with my kids growing up we've build this special bond and feeling around xmas time with getting together with lots of family members was great all those years until xmas last year.

Since March this year along with few other occasions that I've declined and disregarded sadly xmas was one of them occasions that meant nothing to me, it's not that there's nothing to celebrate about but with me there's no interest to celebrate any occasion at all, apart from my kids and my wife I really didn't want to see anyone, especially the useless and the fake people that I've known for a little while and the ones that are responsible for me being in this miserable state around what usually is a beautiful festive season where an ideal thing to do is to get my wife, my kids and a large number of valued family members together to have deliciously prepared lunch and dinner and spend some quality time together like we used to do, but not this year, this year the only two people validates my worth and stood by my side and still standing by my side are my wife and my son.

I would hate to think where would I be without them, so while I'm thinking about all this I am getting emotional, shortness of breath and teary again, the messed up thoughts, mental instability, very little physical ability and the agoraphobia are very powerful and very real and I sometimes strongly feel that it's not going to be over anytime soon, and that worries me and scares me immensely, at the moment I don't know and I can never be sure if I'll ever get over this, this can keep one wandering for a very long time.

December 28, 2019.
Surprise surprise another useless night last night, not much time spent in bed, I know it gets boring constantly thinking and going through the same shit again and again but that's how it is in my everyday life these days, so here I go again, yeah sometimes I wonder if I'm kidding myself by thinking that this is all going to be over soon and I'm going to get my life back to normal again, but I really can't see that happening in the near future.

I wish I could help not being negative about a lot of things all the time but when I can't see anything good in the horizon and there seems to be no light at the end of the tunnel, that's where positivity don't seem to exist, lost soul and at times zombie like with pain killers and the useless antidepressants.

I guess sometimes I should thank my lucky stars that for some reason I'm still holding it together and that I'm able to write my daily thoughts on to a piece of paper so that one day if I ever get over this I can look back and read about all this and maybe be proud of myself, anyway here's more negative stuff that's debilitating me from getting myself out of the darkness is that I'm truly sick and tired of pretending to be okay and happy in the presence of my wife and my son, I'm sick of putting on a false brave face for them so they don't worry about me, the only time I can be myself is when I'm in the corner of the backyard where I don't have to pretend, deep down I'm scared very scared sometimes I feel the end is very near, this feeling absolutely petrifies me.

Knowing that what I want to do or don't want to do no one has any power over me, knowing that when I've stepped on the field of suicidal ideations twice and the actioning or stepping off the field can only be a snap decision, it is a very frightening experience that I personally don't want to see or hear anyone go through it, you see this is a very complex issue and in many cases it's a very brief subject, now when we hear that so and so had committed suicide yes we feel sad and we feel bad and we constantly think that we might have been able to help to prevent it from happening and then we come to a silent conclusion " maybe not" and then we move on yes life goes on no matter what, and with me getting off the field twice I don't know if it was a blessing or if it was the personally created strong policies of mine had over powered the ideations for me not to go through with it.

If I ever get out of this safely one day there's a very good chance I'll be able to confirm as to why I didn't actioned it. With all this in mind how do you talk to anyone about this, oh by the way recently I mentioned to a paid professional of what I heard on the news is that someone in another country took the matters into his own hands and gone to his work place and destroyed the lives of twelve people, I specifically told her that I don't condone it but however I can understand why he did what he did and the response was if I keep thinking and talking like this she'll have no option but to break the confidentiality rule and report me to higher authorities well with me getting this kind of response from a paid professional what chance do I have talking to ordinary people like friends and family members.

With all this in mind this is when someone like me puts themselves in a confined captivity where they easily become agoraphobic and cut off from the outside world, if and when I want to talk to people like friends and family members and knowing their lack of knowledge and understanding of this complex topic and knowing that they are going to tell me everything is going to be alright would feel intimidatingly patronizing and antagonizing so therefore it is quite appropriate to stew privately and silently in my own misery without being a burden on anyone.

Yes, it does become hugely complicated trying to explain to people how real and how powerful this thing I'm going through is at the moment, and yes it is a misunderstood issue or topic if you like.

December 30, 2019.

Beginning of just another useless and fruitless day, what can I say, the presence of what's in my head feels very ghostly, very cold, very dark and very deep it's very real and it is also very hard to shake it off and get rid of, the feeling of being on the tread mill of self destruction is very heavy, the resistance of getting off the tread mill of self destruction becomes totally useless at a lot of times.

The feeling kicks in as if I owe it to the loved and respected ones of my family that I should constantly keep on persisting, pushing and using every strand of my strength to resist the idea of staying on the tread mill of self destruction unvalidatedly, undeserved and without any selfish reasons at all, why am I talking like this always comes down to the people that I've worked with that I've trusted and I've relied on are the prime reasons as to why I found myself where I am today.

Maybe I've placed far too much emphasis unequivocally on these people, maybe this is one of the prime reasons why I am suffering so much and in so much pain mentally, thinking about all this and writing about it is heightening me almost instantly, again shortness of breath and my eyes are full of tears, this is when I need to go outside have a coffee and a couple of cigarettes try to calm down and get my composure back so when I return I can put more of my true feelings down on these pages.

Yeah I've returned almost three hours later, in that three hours I've managed to stay away from mental pressures and physical limited abilities and fears, well six months ago had surgery done on my left shoulder, I've been seeing a physio to the point where it was almost recovered and early this month I've had the surgery done on my left forearm, and now as we speak I have my left arm in bandages in a solid plastic and in a sling, even though the bandages, the plastic and the sling will be removed early next month.

This has created another issue another chapter in my head to worry about, and for some reason I don't believe I'll ever get the full usage of my left shoulder or my left arm again, this in itself is gaining a lot of weight in my mental department to bring me down even lower, apart from everything else the limited usage of my left shoulder and left arm does become a prime concern, simply because I believe I still have over seven years of working life left before I can retire.

It is on my mind that I would dearly love to retire gracefully, mmmm well once again I am optimistically hopeful I guess, now the big question is that if I can't work until my retirement age where the hell do I go and what the hell will I do? Now like everything else all this does become a whirlpool of unanswered questions that pours into the big misery pond of my mind, so there you have it, when I dive into the misery pond I don't have the chance or the opportunity to pick and choose the issues that I deal with on daily basis or sometimes on the hour, and yes I do dive into the misery pond quite a lot.

December 31, 2019.
Today I'm not going to talk about how my night was or how much pain killers and antidepressants I've been consuming, being the last day of the year I was hoping to have a calm day, hoping to have a day where I don't have to pay any attention to anything at all, but unfortunately that's unrealistic and unachievable that's because I keep diving into the misery pond the proper terminology for diving at the moment is falling.

I don't seem to have a choice to be in the misery pond or not, just like now I had unwillingly fallen into the misery pond and when I surfaced here's the topic of the day I'll be dealing with, here it is the rage is increasing the thoughts I'm having right now are out of control, if somebody asks me where is this coming from and why? Simple answer is I don't know, what I'm thinking of right now and what I want to do does not only put me into the state of fear but it's risky and it's dangerous.

Sometimes I don't want to write some of the things that goes through my head but then again if I'm not true to myself and I'm not honest about all this than what is the point about putting all on these this pages? So today I'm thinking about some useless people that I totally dislike.

I would dearly love to see them take their last breath in my presence, I would love to look at their faces and see their eyes shut for the very last time, I am having difficulties breathing now and wasting a lot of good energy trying to keep my rage under control but at the same time still managing to entertain the dangerous thoughts in my head, still thinking that it would give me the greatest satisfaction and it would make everything okay and my life would be back to normal again very quickly, how nice that would feel, that's if don't end up in jail or the other alternative is that I go down with them.

As I said I'm only entertaining the idea, I don't want to put any of it into action now and I hope I don't find myself in a situation without an option, for the rest of the day and night before I go into the new year I need to constantly remind myself of how much my family means to me and I need to constantly keep on drumming into my head the difference between leaving or staying, and the impact, the sadness and the financial burden and so on.

If I'm honest and truthful about how much my family means to me so why would I put them through all this misery on my unacceptable decision that was made in the heat of the moment where I'm full of rage and incredibly heightened, well out of all this there's one positive thing I've learned, not long ago I used to think and worry about what other people would think or say, if I've actioned anything they would call me an idiot, coward, silly and selfish maybe more but now I don't think or care about other people's assumptions or opinions, so I want to finish the last day and the last night of the year with some optimism I want to hope and pray for some positivity in my life, I need and want to have a better year, I want to make some good memories rather than living with hopeless dreams.

I want to be free from all this misery, I wish I could find the genuine ability to forgive some of these people, knowing that the one who forgives can benefit a lot more than the one that's forgiven.

January 1, 2020.
Yeah starting a brand new year with continuation of the old misery attached to it, how wonderful, new years eve yesterday I wish I could say how great it was last night and that we had so much fun, yeah well far from it, with the debilitating condition of my left shoulder and my left forearm being in bandages and sling and no changes in the mental state can be quite depleting and it seriously effects the tolerance levels with anything and with anyone.

For instance last night instead of mingling and having fun with family and close friends my wife and I watched TV and welcomed the new year with tears in my eyes not knowing how long is this going to go on for.

Looking forward to full physical recovery of my left shoulder and left forearm but with the strong uncertainty of what percentage of usage I will regain? unknown, if I don't get the full usage of my shoulder and arm employment ways where will I end up? Unknown.

How will I control or manage my mental instability? Unknown, with all this in mind we talk about new year resolutions, well here's mine I would like to categorize all my issues and then put them in order where I can deal with them one at a time, even that's questionable not knowing if it can be achievable but no harm in hoping and wishing I guess.

Hey it's almost midnight I just remembered to mention about the pain and the frustration since the first surgery on my left shoulder six months ago and then the second surgery on my left arm last month, now more than six months I still can't sleep on my left side and with the combination of pain killers and the antidepressants I find myself being constipated more often so therefore I take other medication so I can go to the toilet, and quite often I am in constant fear that I will walk in to the walls, doors or the door jams which I have done few times before and in doing that obviously the pain escalates to highest levels where I react terribly and the colourful language comes out of my mouth with high volumes is not pretty at all.

I can feel that I'm not pleasant to be around, so this gives agoraphobia more reasons to settle itself in me and stay with me for who knows how long, so right now instead of going to bed and try to get a good night sleep I will be going out into the backyard to have some coffees and unlimited amount of cigarettes and maybe once again watch the night become a brand new day, and the reason for that is my mind is all over the place again thinking that no one has any idea at all of what's been happening in the last nine months.

it gives me this cold acceptance that no one genuinely cares, so yes I truly do appreciate the tireless effort my wife and my son puts in to being by my side, anyway before the sadness deepens and the tears uncontrollably rolling down my face I have to leave it here with the thought that tomorrow is a brand new day so if there's a chance of me convincing myself to be optimistic about some goodness ahead on my path I will, I guess it won't hurt.

January 2, 2020.

I've made about three attempts to go to bed last night and wanted to get a good night sleep, well it didn't work for me but at least I was able to view the beginning of a new day, and about last night I'm starting to run out of strong pain killers so I'm on the light headache tablets which are useless by the way.

If I don't move my arm so much the pain can be manageable but being in the same position all the time does get a bit annoying, including the elbow and my forearm are all bandaged and placed in a hard plastic so there's no movement on my left arm and being in the middle of the summer doesn't help at all, inside the bandages it gets itchy and sweaty, I can't scratch it and I can't wipe it so that becomes another reason to be angry again.

Anyway, without going too much into my despair I would like to think that I'm patiently doing okay, waiting till next week for the bandages to be removed something to look forward to I guess, so now I'm starting to except that there are lots of rocky roads ahead in terms of physical and mental recovery processes but for the moment I'm still unsure of what percentage of movement will I get on my left shoulder and my left forearm and for my mental instability?

Well I don't know and I don't believe there's anyone out there that can give me any indication or any direction on how soon or how will I ever get out of this miserable mess, I know it is a battle, I also know that I don't want to fight an unwinnable battle, I truly don't want this frustration anymore.

I really would like to get my head in a good space again and physically I do want to get better, I do want to drive again, I want to do the things I used to do and most importantly I want to enjoy life and my family again, but like I said there's still a lot of stormy days ahead, I wish I could promise myself that I will do my best, if I can't go forward at least remain where I am for the moment and stay out of trouble.

January 3, 2020.

My wife drove me to my mum's this morning, it's always great to see my mum, in her presence there's no judgement, no nonsense questions, no intimidations, no patronizing in any way, just a pure heart to heart great conversations about everything else except my misery.

I guess I don't want my mum to worry about me after all it is my job to worry about her in her tender and delicate age, anyhow back home about midday and it's same old same old until I go to bed, sleep? Well that's another issue, still find myself outside in the backyard around two or three am and so on.

I guess I just can't help myself, once I wake up I realize that I've woken up with all this shit spinning around and around in my head to a point where I feel I've been dictated to get a coffee grab my cigarettes and run outside to try and sort it all out, yeah well good luck with that, it doesn't happen instantaneously, instead quite often I find myself being pulled into the pond of misery where the dangerous thoughts start to pop up from every corner of my mind, and suddenly I find myself on the treadmill of self destruction again.

I am doing my best not to entertain any of these dangerous thoughts or self harm ideations, oh yes I am scared and I am worried that the pilot light is always on and it can ignite at any given time without any warning, I don't know how it happens but when I get in to these thoughts I begin to have breathing difficulties and become teary to the point where I start to cry like a little boy and I start to feel sad and sorry for myself, that's where I find myself slipping further down into the darkness in a very difficult place where it takes days just to stand let alone climbing onto a surface where I might have a chance to see things differently or a bit more clearly but that doesn't happen easily these days,

I can't write anymore I'm tired very tired, I just want this nightmare to end instantly I'm so over it, I just want it all to go away now, I'm almost done with all this.

January 6, 2020.

Seen the psychologist this morning, taxi there and back with the generosity of the insurer because I can't drive yet, anyhow the counselling wasn't bad at all today, we spoke about the surgery done on my left arm.

I've explained to her with the reduction of pain on my left shoulder and my left arm obviously I've reduced the excessive consumption of pain killers but when I mention to her about the antidepressants making me angry, making me feel useless, making me less tolerable to anything around me and feeling zombie like

I don't know if she heard me or paid any attention to anything I've just told her, but to my shock I don't know if her reply was manifestly fabricated but without any due consideration she strongly advised me to continue with the antidepressants, well after having quite a few sessions with her it feels like we still don't have a clear direction as to where we're travelling and what sort of tools does my condition require.

I understand that I shouldn't have such a harsh opinion or assumption about some of these medical professionals, I also understand that they have a legal commitment to achieve what needs to be achieved on medical terms.

Before I left the session I mentioned that even though I have lesser physical pain which is manageable for the moment and with the mental issues of where I am right now and that I am finding it very hard to forgive and forget the people who are responsible for me being here and for some family members and some friends I truly don't have any respect and I don't want them near me.

I could have kept going on and on but her reply was that we have came to the end of our session and she will be on annual leave so my next session will be on the third of February, wow mmmm, on the way home few things came to mind, my condition is not important enough not serious enough.

Maybe I should be happy or she just didn't have enough time for me because she was too busy organizing her holidays, and then the angry and the frustrated thoughts started to enter my mind, do I have to put any of the ideations into action to be taken notice of? Let's face it the reason we see a professional is to get a professional help, advice or some kind of tools to get us out of this mess, it is poor and it is giving me a strong discouragement that mental well being is not achievable, maybe this is a powerfully unfair opinion but sometimes I feel I have no other option to think and feel this way.

When I arrived home I received a call from Miss X firstly she tried to show some concern which was very brief and then it was all about how to get me back to work as soon as possible, just to remind you that my arm is still in a sling, I don't know if she's aware but boy can she be pushy I almost want slap her a couple of times to bring her down to earth, I don't know what sort of a carrot is dangling in front of her face to get me back to work but she really needs to tone it down and be a lot more professional about her occupation with compassion and duty of care attached.

In saying that though I am somewhat worried about her attitude because some day she will came across some one that will be less tolerable then me and she could get hurt, anyway she insisted to come with me on Wednesday to see the surgeon to get some solid information as to when can I get back to work, and as I mentioned before though my left arm is still in a sling, well we'll see what happens on the eighth of this month.

January 7, 2020.
Again I don't want to talk about last night, I'm sick and tired of it all myself, It's the same old shit that can really add to my depression to keep me in the dark place for a long long time, however I'm counting the minutes for tomorrow's appointment with the surgeon to get the bandages off.

A bit of a mixed feelings here, on one hand I'm looking forward to the freedom from the pain on my left shoulder and my arm and on the other hand I'm wandering how long before I get the full usage of both the arm and the shoulder and what percentage.

With a lot of help from the physio and I guess I need to rely on time and patience, just another unknown for now, but I can only hope that one day I will get all my priorities in order one way or another, yeah in saying all that I still feel there's a long way to go yet.

January 8, 2020.
Seen the surgeon this morning, first time since the surgery on my left arm, once the surgeon removed the bandages of my arm there was a big sigh of relief.

He has assured me that the surgery went well, after the surgeon instructing me on what to do and what not to do and making a new appointment to see him again on the fifth of February we finally called Miss X to come in to surgeons office.

As per usual no concern from Miss X for my aches and pains and definitely no concern for my mental instability, with her it was straight to the point of almost interrogating the surgeon, bombarding him with questions of the movement of my forearm

How soon can I start using my left arm and most importantly how soon can I get back to work, I have noticed that even the surgeon was getting a bit annoyed and somewhat intimidated by her presence and her unwarranted questions at this point, so with her unprofessional conduct and useless persistence I am starting to get intimidated and aggravated with the feeling of being harassed to the point of losing control.

Okay. not so pleasant things are starting to go through my mind, I am not a violent person but I can be pushed to a limit where I can lose it, it's been done before, but at this point of my life I truly don't need any unnecessarily added legal issues on top of what I'm already dealing with.

Anyhow once the consultation was completed Miss X and I left the surgeons clinic and in front of the clinic while I'm waiting for a taxi we had a brief chat and again it was all about me getting back to work, by this stage I could really feel my aggravation and frustration levels are rising to almost maximum point where I really wanted to grab her head and ram it into the brick wall where the outcome would not have been so good.

The way I felt at this very moment that she would have been left there beyond recognition. Yes, I need to control my hyper aggressive moods and my hyper verbal vocabulary, anyway it didn't stop there when I arrived home luckily my wife wasn't home and with me still being very heightened I went into the backyard where I broke some things and done some damage, again I'm lucky that my son is a carpenter/builder where he repaired everything without any fuss, yeah I was thankful.

So the point to all this is that instead of me concentrating heavily on my physical recovery process and peacefully try and bring my mental pressure down where I can start to climb out of this darkness, instead I'm dealing with some professionals misconduct, luckily I'm not on the edge at this point but if I was to action anything with her misconduct and unprofessionalism would have been enough to push me over the edge, if that's ever happened to anyone out there and they sadly lost their lives we will never know.

I might have mentioned this before that a lot of times I find myself running very low on patience department and I feel that I use far too much of my inner strength dealing with people that don't understand the serious consequences of their unprofessional actions. Oh by the way when my wife arrived home I sheepishly tried to explain to her that the damage in the backyard was an accident but I don't think she believed me and by the look on her face I could tell that she wasn't able to hide her concern for me.

Anyway, I know that silence can be an emotional oppression that's why I try and put everything that's on my mind onto these pages.

January 14, 2020.
I've seen the physio this morning, she started on my left arm rubbed some cream on it however the movement was very limited on the left arm and shoulder so I think in the next two to three weeks of physio I am optimistically hopeful that we will get some range of movement and lifting the arm to a comfortable levels.

I didn't write anything the last few days, I've been doing a lot of useless thinking again, one of my strong and heavy thoughts were how Miss X treated me and the surgeon last Wednesday when the bandages was removed.

I just can't shake off the way she conducted herself and how totally unacceptable her behaviour was that it really disturbed me, and I'm still trying to understand how the hell did I control myself in her presence last Wednesday, looking back now and been thinking about it last few days that I think she has seen the anger and the rage in my face on that day that she couldn't get away quick enough from me.

I think it was the best think she's done on that day, I feel the need to stop right here right now, I can feel the rage escalating just thinking about it, I need to go outside to get some air, having difficulty breathing again.

January 16, 2020.
2.45am this morning feeling uncomfortable with my left arm and shoulder so got out of bed went outside to have few coffees and cigarettes.

I don't feel like going back to bed so I'll sit here and write some of the things that goes through my mind that keeps me awake most nights, so the pain killers and the sleeping pills are not as effective anymore, maybe there's an element of disagreement with the antidepressants I am consuming at the same time, I wouldn't know as I am not a medical professional, guinea pig maybe.

Well, I do follow the instructions of every medical professional that's on my case thinking that they are there to help me to recover, well I guess it can be debatable but I don't want to go into it right now, another issue another time maybe.

It's 4.20 am now and I'm still questioning a lot of things, and one of them is my left shoulder I've had the surgery done seven months ago and I still have limited usage, still can't sleep on my left side and I still feel considerable amount of pain trying to lift my left arm above my shoulder level, and then my left forearm.

I know it's only been six weeks I still can't make a full fist, and I only have between ten to fifteen percent usage of both left shoulder and forearm, I'm struggling to tie up my shoe laces, getting dressed, brushing my teeth and many other daily activities, I sure do feel debilitated where my wife helps me out with some of these activities, while I go through the physical and debilitating side of my issues on daily basis every day I still think about how all this started and how it was handled in my work place together with my team members, doctors, all the medical professionals and the insurance company, and how I've been given a lot of running around to prove to everyone that I had genuine work injuries on my left shoulder and my left forearm and in the process I've been made to feel a liar, fake, dishonest and untruthful I have proof of some this untrue and disrespectful sledging.

I could not have been that bad of a person where early January twenty nineteen I have received two gifts from one of my managers for xmas telling me how good I was controlling the loading bays and everyone was happy with me leading my team, so go figure, so when my ordeal started mid March twenty nineteen within four weeks I've become suicidal in fact I've tried it twice in the same year.

I guess the opprobrium that was piled on me become too much to handle, even though I use a lot of my strength to keep the lid on suicidal ideations but I wish I could find the way to put out the pilot light for good, it feels like it is impossible at the moment but life goes on and it must go on.

I need to get over my agoraphobia and get out my confined isolation to go on with my life if I can, I just don't want to go through my life with illusion of content

January 21, 2020.
Seen the physio this morning, she done what she does best I had no interest, there was no communicational efforts made by me, if she asked anything my reply was short and sharp.

I did apologize before I left the clinic, Today like the last four days I feel overwhelmed, disappointed, unhappy and indecisive I feel sad that I'm going through all this emotional bull shit that I don't deserve and I don't need so here I go breaking down and crying like a little boy again.

I can feel a long afternoon and night coming along maybe running into the early hours of tomorrow morning, I would like to think that I'm strong enough to deal with it as long as I stay in my confined isolation

January 23, 2020.
Up and out of bed very early this morning straight out into the backyard with my coffee and cigarettes, well coffee and cigarettes are the best company at the moment they can also be the best tools and good medicine.

I don't feel like writing anymore it's all the same bull shit over and over again that I'm just so sick and tired of it all, I'm still popping pain killers together with the useless antidepressants, still can't sleep on my left side.

I still don't believe I'm ever going to get the full usage of my left shoulder and my arm, I still don't have faith in my near and distant future, still have a lot of questions going around and around in my head and still don't associate with people, now I'm getting more and more angry writing about all this, it mysteriously reignites all the bull shit in my head, it all makes me start entertaining the idea of revenge again, it scares me that I'm thinking of some nasty revenging actions without thinking of any consequences.

I know one thing for sure that sometimes it is so hard to control and so hard to get that revengeful ideas out of my head and it is extremely hard to try and act normal, it is getting harder and harder to live with illusional contentment.

January 28, 2020.
Another restless night, up and out of bed at all different hours of early mornings just like I've been doing the last few days.

The only different activity today to get me out of the house is that I've attended my physio appointment which again was a very small baby steps, however even if it's forcefully done I feel that I have no option but to keep the physical recovery hopefulness alive in my head and in my heart, on the other hand though I get puzzled very puzzled on how I'm managing mentally.

At times I get this very small pleasant feeling that I'm doing okay and most importantly I'm still here on this earth writing about all this and one day sharing it with whoever is interested in my true events that I've been going through and god only knows how long more will I be going through it so with my physical activities being so limited enables me to spend a lot of time in my agoraphobic confinement that I do a lot of thinking.

Here's another one that I've been stewing on lately, when you're in a burnt out state it is almost an impossible task to try and rekindle what's already burnt and turned into ashes, in order to restart the fire again you need kindling's, firewood, coal and so on, but with me being in isolation since March twenty nineteen and in an agoraphobic state that I truly don't know if and when will I ever start that fire again to reenergize, reinvigorate or recuperate my life

My worth and my purpose again, yeah I guess I can think of all these things but at the end of my long and painful thoughts about all this is that there's no resolution, no solution, no direction, no manifestation and no fabrication of finding my way back to where I was all my life, but now it always looks and feels like a dead end and there's no way out, but I'm hoping that one day this will all be figured out for me or hopefully I will have the ability to figure it out for myself

January 31, 2020.
Up early again this morning, surprise surprise yes coffees and cigarettes since about two forty five am, six fifteen at the moment, feel flat and negative for just about everything, I just don't know how to start my day, I have absolutely no desire to do anything at all, as usual I just want to stay at home.

I have no interest to communicate with anyone, just neutral at the moment, I don't want to even think about anything, I think deep down for all these tired emotions today is that I don't want to reignite any negative thoughts in my head where it drifts me into sad, ugly, angry and revengeful fantasies, so because of these sadly negative thoughts in my head is the reason why I'm becoming more and more withdrawn from people in general, besides there's really no one out there that you can have a decent conversation with and if there is they are the ones that get paid handsomely whether they understand you or not but they listen.

Anyhow, I'm still here and it's 10.30am now and the wife is at her mum's, for me it's more alone time to do more thinking and more writing, I can feel the weight and the heaviness of this emotion of feeling totally blank, useless and worthless.

I truly wish there was a simple way of snapping out of all this, I now know the meaning of loneliness and I am starting to understand more and more why certain people put an end to it all and I am also getting to know and understand the pretenders and the shit talkers.

Well I am one of the pretenders I guess and I do pretend to be happy in the presence of the ones I love and respect, making sure that they see me okay and that there's nothing to worry about me, as hard as it is to pretend I do feel I have no choice.

I simply don't want anyone to see me in my misery and I don't want anyone to worry for me, and then there are the shit talkers, they ask you if you're okay but before you have a chance to speak or answer any of their questions they very quickly take over the conversation and start saying things like they know exactly how you are feeling because someone they know went through the same thing and it goes on and on, and then I find myself wandering WTF!! Just happened, people have no knowledge but they powerfully become so opinionated that they are trying to tell you how to suck eggs, so you can understand my dilemma why I want to be alone in my own miserable environment, hey I'm getting used to it.

Then there are those who whisper sweet nothings into your ear, they tell you they are going to spend some quality time with you, they are going to take you to cafes or restaurants to get you away from your misery even if it's short periods, or they will take you away for the weekend, well it's been ten months and I'm still waiting for these gunners and lip service givers, never mind, we all know that when the sun comes up it comes up for everyone.

As we can all deal with some form of dilemma in our lives, anyway I think that's enough of resentment, regrets, hatred and anger for today, it's only eleven fifteen am I think I'll go and get another coffee and my cigarettes go outside to call it a day in silence.

February 3, 2020.

Just another night and just another day ahead trying to focus and stay focused throughout the day, thank god for my coffees and cigarettes.

Yeah I know I keep mentioning my coffees and cigarettes but hey I guess I could do worst things like alcohol or illicit hard substances to see me through the day and night, luckily I haven't resourced in any of these avenues yet.

Anyhow, seen the psychologist this morning, we primarily spoke about Miss X and how she treated me and the surgeon early last month, after me explaining to the psychologist exactly what had happened and how angry I felt at the time and how things could have turned ugly, but even though she showed some concern yet she hasn't given me anything to take home and work on, the only sure thing I've got out of today's session was that she gave four new appointments until the end of March.

Today's session felt like was a poor excuse to get me out of the house, does this leave me scratching my head yes!! Does this make me feel lost yes it does and it leaves me with the question of what's the point of these sessions, I don't know.

I was referred to these sessions by my family doctor backed up by the WI Dr, again taxi there and back, wow how exiting, so in other words I feel the same now as I did before the session today, well this is another one of those instructions I follow so diligently but whether it's helping me or not doesn't seem to matter, yeah it makes me wander too, is it the only time all this will matter if I try and do something so drastic, again I don't know.

For the rest of the day and night? Well yes you've guessed it same old same old, the stew of the old misery and I think you know all the ingredients by now.

February 4, 2020

Physio this morning, in reality even though I do what I have to do with the physio today the baby steps doesn't feel like they are enlarging at all, maybe I shouldn't be too hard on myself.

Maybe I should except that I simply can't achieve miracles in just one week, maybe I should be able to control myself not to become so discouraged, I'm sure the physio is doing her job to the best of her ability, maybe I am becoming impatient.

This is just one of the issues that becomes inflated and enlarged in my head with all the other half or fully inflated issues where it becomes incredibly hard and at times almost impossible to control or to deal with, these are the times when I consider each of my issues as an avenue for me to enter to solve and get a positive resolution where it turns out to be a dead end after dead end, and often enough it feels like a black hole ready to explode.

This is what I commonly deal with on daily basis, however though I don't want to lose hope and I don't want to lose my optimism, I need and want to believe that I will one day overcome my issues, I will continue my journey towards my destination peacefully and lovingly, again no harm in dreaming I guess

February 5, 2020.
Up and out of bed early again this morning, yeah I'm sounding like a broken record but then again this really is a regular occurrence in my everyday life these days.

I do feel compelled to truly and honestly write down my every thought and every activity minute by minute on the hope that it might help somebody someday, in my agoraphobic state where I spend a lot of time in the same spot here's another idea that's been going around in my head, it's not a joke and I hope that it won't become a laughing matter so here it is, I am feeling the strong need to develop an imaginary skill an ability to shrink myself, make myself become a micro man so that I can enter into my mental cavity.

Once I'm in I'd like to look at it as a large storeroom or a big warehouse where I can carefully and selectively condense all my issues into small boxes than label them put a sticky tape on them all and then carefully stack them onto pallets nice and neat, once that's done I'll get out of there, and then whenever I get the opportunity I can re-enter that warehouse peacefully and calmly to deal with all my issues one box at a time, in the hope that I will get great results, yeah wouldn't that be great in the ideal world if it can be achievable.

As I've mentioned before in the mental and physical recovery process I do have too much time on my hands that enables me to think too much, some of the things I think of can sometimes be silly, sometimes can be embarrassing quite often annoying.

Sometimes I feel it might have some importance to what I'm thinking but unable to make any solid decisions remembering and sadly excepting that I'm not in a right state of mind to make any decision and whatever documents comes from any of the medical professionals is a good thing that it all comes through emails or letters they are sent by post so that I can take my time reading it carefully and analysing the information before I can reply, quick reply or making decisions on the spot are things in the past so it feels at the moment, so that's embarrassing.

People can tell me not to feel like this and not to feel embarrassed, easy said than done, how true, anyway seen the surgeon this morning about my left forearm, he asked me to move my arm in a few directions and me openly telling him how I felt and unless I move my arm up and down or side to side there's no pain to be concerned about and that when I'm resting it there's no pain at all and that the pain is quite manageable with reduced amount of pain killers.

The surgeon was happy with all that and told me to keep doing what I'm doing with the physio and he'll see me again on the forth of March, taxi there and back and that was my outing for the day, sometimes the taxi drivers can get a bit annoying they just want to talk and talk and sometimes it's great all we say to each other is hello and good bye, seriously though if a person is going to see a surgeon, psychiatrist, psychologist or even a family doctor as a taxi driver why the hell would you make that person feel like he/she has being interrogated.

Actually a couple of times I've pretended that I was on the phone so that I don't have to communicate in saying that though I'm not happy nor am I proud it's quite the opposite, before my ordeal started I could talk to anybody about anything, yeah that's another issue unattended in my head momentarily, however I will attend to it and resolve it when the time is right.

February 6, 2020.

No, nope, not today, I don't want to talk about my night last night and my morning and how I got out of bed and what time and how many coffees and cigarettes I've had, no. Instead I just want to give it all a rest,

I don't want to think and I don't want to talk today at all if I can help it, I had an appointment with the WI Dr today, I don't know why but she told me that she wanted to know how I'm travelling mentally and physically if I'm recovering quickly and satisfactorily that we can start talking about my return to work program, well it is at a point in my mind that no matter what I say, what I do or how I feel both mentally or physically is that it has no validity.

The way some of these medical professionals look, talk and listen to you, you can almost tell that whatever you're saying to them is not registering, it feels like it's already been manifested and return to work program is already been organized and when the indicated time arrives you will be made to go back to work unless you have a valid reason that you simply can't, I guess it's just a waiting game now, we'll see what happens, and the rest of the day and night, again same old same old.

February 7, 2020.

Today I had an appointment with my family Doctor at two forty pm, for an annual check up, I've missed it, apart from being totally blank and I don't give a rats attitude I think lunch time might have a lot to do with it.

I was trying to help my wife setting the table at lunch time with me being over confident I grabbed two plates with food one on each hand and started to walk from the kitchen to the dining table, but the pain on my left forearm became so excruciating that I had to drop the plate off of my left hand, obviously made a bit of a mess on the floor and with my wife being so kind and understanding where all this left me with my emotions being elevated to a point leaving me with no other option but to go out into the backyard with escalated pain in my forearm and crying like a little boy again.

It's not that I look for an excuse or a reason to cry, I've never been so weak in the emotional part of my life but these days the tears are not controllable, I just can't help myself, one thing I'm pleased about today's mishap is that my hyper verbal and colourful vocabulary was not activated.

Anyway, about the annual check up with my family doctor will happen at another time when I feel up to it, yeah it is important for an annual check up I guess especially these days with me drinking excessive amounts of coffees and irregular meals and meal times and not to mention the cigarettes, yes I will make the appointment soon, and yep you've guessed it the rest of the day and night same old same old.

I am trying to stay away from the negative thoughts in my head, not succeeding but I'm trying.

February 8, 2020.
No point in writing about last night or this morning, nothing new, nothing enlivened, and nothing exhilarating just been blank and motionless about everything.

Not seeing any light at the end of my tunnel and definitely nothing in the horizon and not even an illusional contentment of life, definitely not a good way to live but for whatever the reason we make our self's believe that life goes on and it must, and just as I am stewing in my misery in one of those deepest and darkest hour looking for a rope or some steps to bring me back out of my darkness and onto a surface where there's a bit of light.

I've received a phone call from my daughter, she has given me the greatest news of a lifetime telling me that I'm going to be a granddad for the first time, oh what a news just when I needed it, I could feel myself frozen momentarily, in and around my life every think is at a standstill, the tears are flowing endlessly, as I started to regain my composure the first thing came to my mind in the form of wander or question I'm not sure, is that is this a miracle? Is this going to be enough to deter me away from any of my hair rising and dangerous ideations? Is this the time I lower my guards? And is this the time where I store my weapons away temporarily or for good?

Wow so many new questions, again struggling with answers, mixed emotions tears are still flowing down my face, oh by the way the reason I haven't mentioned my daughter before is that she lives over two thousand kilometres away in interstate with her partner and now with a new baby on the way building a future together, so it's the last thing I would do to burden her with my issues, I simply don't want her to worry about me and all this time I made sure that my wife or my son don't give her any information about what I'm going through, she might know about five percent and that's more than enough for me.

Anyhow, back to the mixed emotions and questions again, and as the tears rolling down my face here's the final question I paid a lot of attention for the rest of the day and night, is this grandchild of mine going to be enough for me to change my direction? My way of thinking? am I going to be able to forgive and forget the people that are reasonable for my misery?

Am I ever going to except where I am with or without my imperfections ? do I get to enjoy the rest of my journey? And will I get to my final destination naturally? Even though the tears of joy are rolling down my face but for some reason it is over clouded and over shadowed by all these questions that have no immediate, no solid and no satisfying answers, anyway without going any further about all the negativities I'll just go and enjoy the good news as long as I can, while I can.

February 10, 2020.
When you're living with an emotional oppression twenty four seven it is hard it's so hard that it makes you become someone that you're not proud of, even though it's against your strong policies it makes you feel that you've became a social reject simply because you don't want to associate with anyone, well rightfully so one would think because there's no one to talk to no one to share what you're going through.

As a matter of fact once not long ago I was sharing my true thoughts with someone on social media, oh it felt great I thought we have some similarities until one of the well known organizations that was supposed to help people with depression actually asked me not to associate with anyone about my issues on social medi.

This kind of attitude from so called expert organizations had instantly confirmed my distrust and my levels of confidence to speak to any of them went right down, well the question rises again, if you can't speak to anyone in any of these expert organizations who can you really speak to or rely on?

This is when I find this invisible force that's powerfully pushing me deeper and deeper into my agoraphobic state that not only I don't want to talk to people but I don't even want to see them as well, and when I do come back home from any of my appointments and I find myself in my confinement there's always a big sigh of relief that I'm in my own safe environment, even though I'm trying to be optimistic and hopeful while I'm trying to do my best to get me out of this useless state that I'm in but quite often I find if I take three steps forward and then something happens with one of my medical professionals or the insurer that takes me back four to five steps backwards, at the moment it's at a point where it's inevitable that it happens just about every time, and then I remind myself It is what is and that life goes on.

Anyhow, I've seen the psychologist this morning again with the generosity of the insurer I've had a taxi there and back, again the counselling session today was not satisfactory, I felt that we were fishing a lot, even though I've mentioned some of the above thoughts there was no valid reply, I feel we're still not making any grounds here and I still don't have a solid direction as to where I'm going or am I making any progress? Yeah sometimes it makes me wonder if these counselling sessions was made to become a protocol instigated by some government bodies together with some insurance companies carefully programmed and turned into a standard operating procedures regardless of the outcome, okay maybe I shouldn't be so harshly critical I don't mean to offend anyone, if I do I'm sorry, that's what I think and that's what I feel right now.

I'm finding it very hard to control my thoughts, when something comes to my mind I can chew on it for hours, simply because I have the time, after the counselling session this morning I also seen my family doctor for an annual check up he gave me a referral for a blood test early Friday morning, for the rest of the day and I do a lot more of thinking while I'm in a physical recovery process and doing my best to keep a lid on my emotions, I need to be safe and I need to be away from unnecessary problems and troubles.

February 11, 2020.

Physio again this morning, the physical recovery is positive and on the rise but boy it's slow, at times I think it's smaller than baby steps, but I'm not about to give up.

I feel I need to use my mental and physical strength mainly on my recoveries, not on negatively dangerous ideations of any kind, before all this started I know I've had the strength I know

I've had the power to do anything, I also know my abilities and my capabilities and when I talk about my capabilities I know I can powerfully use it both ways, good or bad and that really worries me, some of the things I was capable of doing and done in the past even now shockingly amazes me, so thinking about all this puts a fear in me, you see the reason I'm writing about all my true feelings and my sad or happy thoughts on these pages is that I don't talk to anyone I don't talk to any of the highly paid expert organizations.

I can honestly tell you that all these experts in those luxurious offices are employed with handsome salaries and expensive company vehicles, the expertise of these people is like on a cold dark windy night they are trying to shine a light on your path with a naked candle, what I feel like telling these people is hey get a f$%^ing torch might go a long way, and right now thinking and writing about all this is really making me angry to a point where I can scream, I can throw punches, I can kick and even pull the trigger without any hesitations and no concern for any consequences, this is where the area in my mind that controls my capability department becomes overheated.

Another reason why I'm talking about all this is I've attended my appointment with the psychiatrist this afternoon, after getting the formality of asking each other briefly of how we are out of the way, he told me that I am mentally not ready for employment until after the fifth of March and then he gave me two forms for me to email them to whoever needs them, so my session with the psychiatrist was just that, after seeing me for just ten minutes gloating with triumph and thinking that he gave me all the guidance, tools and assurance that I needed for my mental wellbeing and mental recovery I left his office totally disappointed and dissatisfied and once again coming home scratching my head and wandering what was the f$%#ing point?

Anyway, when I arrived home I have this hesitancy about emailing these forms to Miss X the liaison lady, knowing how devoted she is to get me back to work the information on these two forms will not be appreciated too kindly by her and she'll be rising my frustration levels very high again. And guess what I was right she wasn't happy about it and she told me that she'll get back to me about me going back to my employment on light duties on Thursday the thirteenth, we'll see what miracle performances she has in store for me, so as if I don't have enough on my plate right now the last thing I need now is for someone like Miss X to put more shit on it simply because she needs to prove something or justify her existence in the firm that she is poorly employed.

Maybe I should stop here about Miss X because paying too much useless attention to her and her activities is fuelling my rage, as much as I'm trying to do my best and not to reveal too much on these pages about certain people that if anything goes wrong I might be held responsible, at the moment I don't want that and I don't need that, so I'm just going to leave it here and see what happens in the next few days.

February 12, 2020.

Once again there's too much happening in my days with medical professionals and Miss X that I don't want to talk about my nights and early mornings about me being in physical pain and mental pressure, where I constantly use my cigarettes and coffees as my main tools to reduce some mental pressure so that I can remain calm and don't do anything unacceptable, not easy but no other choice at the moment.

Anyhow, I constantly sit here and think of distractions to deter me away from unidealistic thoughts and activities, here's one of those distractions, eight am this morning I was at my family clinic getting a blood test for an annual check up, this is just another sad and sorry activity I do once a year and when the results are in I go into the doctor's office to be told to stop smoking, stop eating fried foods and get told that I have cholesterol issues, well I'm not dead yet I've been doing this for the last eleven years, well just another formality I guess.

Anyhow, I've heard from the work injury doctor [WI Dr] early this morning about return to work program, we were on the phone about fifteen minutes, I think she was confused about Miss X's persistence and fiery push about the swift return to work program for me that left her uncomfortable and annoyed and in that fifteen minute conversation on the phone we've achieved nothing and we didn't know what to do, so we thought we'll leave it to Miss X and we'll wait to hear from her, so sure enough not long after that I've received a call from Miss X telling me that after the fifth of March once we've received the reports from the forearm surgeon and the psychiatrist and then Miss X, WI Dr and myself will get together to have a conference meeting to decide my future prospective about my employment, nothing about tomorrow's trial basis return to work with my current employer.

I'll wait and see what happens tomorrow, while all this is happening I've received a call from one of the officials from the insurer, once I've explained to her of what was going on today she was also puzzled and did not know what to do but at the same time she has organized a taxi for me to go to work and back tomorrow, wow I'm in the control or the management of these professionals and everyone is puzzled and yet I still don't know if I'm going to work tomorrow or not, however I will give the surgeon some credit that he has given me a clearance to return to work on light duties providing I don't lift with my left arm and I don't do any work above shoulder level so he has done his job, and the psychiatrist does not see me fit to return to work for mental reasons obviously but Miss X cannot except psychiatrist's diagnostic report for some reason.

I am not a medical expert nor am I a legal expert but from what I can understand that Miss X is leaving herself totally wide open for a serious law suit, the reason I'm saying this is I've only revealed maybe twenty percent of what goes through my head on the basis of hatred, resentment, violence and anger to the psychiatrist, him being the professional that he is maybe he picked up on the other eighty percent of what I may be capable of, and it would be a good idea if Miss X was made aware of that and she needs to be told to get out of my radar, so once again as if I didn't have enough on my plate I've got to deal with all this uselessness as well, the only difference here is that I am the victim and I don't get paid handsomely for putting up with all this bull shit.

February 13, 2020.
Up and out of bed early this morning yeah usual stuff, coffees and cigarettes the only difference this morning is that I'm still puzzled and still don't know if I'm going to work this morning on a trial basis.

In the mean time, yes you've guess it right more nervousness more anxious and more coffees and more cigarettes, I was supposed to be at work this morning at nine thirty am, at the moment it's eleven thirty am now and I'm still waiting to hear from someone to give me some confirmation as to what's happening, some direction of where am I going.

When things like this happens it becomes another blow to my mental area, and it feels like another step or two into the deep and darkness where it already feels impossible to eliminate these issues to rise and see the light, so as usual I'll just sit here and keep on stewing in my defenceless state and getting more and more frustrated and people want to know why am I so angry.

Anyway, I think I'll leave it for now, I'm sweating and I'm having difficulties breathing, I am contemplating on doing some terrible stuff today, but I will restrain myself and stay at home, I think it will be the best I can do today.

February 14, 2020.
Home alone again all day and all night, still no news from any of the professionals who are very committed and very interested in sending me back to work with no consideration of how I feel what so ever.

Sitting here not knowing what's happening no one's been in touch with me about my return to work inevitably creates some dark clouds above my head, it is almost a silent confirmation that no one cares or gives a rats arse, just like some of the narcissistic people I've worked with the last eleven years, no contact with any of them, but on the other hand knowing that I've associated with these people diminishes my integrity and my faith in humanity and with some people I'm still associating and with some I'm yet to associate with, now talking about Miss X I think she finds my psychiatrist to be a real professional on his field and very educated that she finds it extremely hard to manipulate and intimidate him, so the poor thing, she must be getting frustrated as well, well come to my world Miss X.

Oh well, until I hear from Miss X, the insurer, the psychiatrist or the WI Dr I'll just sit here and wait for instructions, yeah it's hard and frustrating not being able to take a step forward in a state of unknown, especially the predicament I'm in mainly mentally, and physically I would like to think that at least I'm half way there, and sometimes as it is very rare I do go to the shops and see someone that I know, when they see the fake and meaningless smile on my face automatically puts them under misapprehension that everything is okay and that I'm doing wel.

With peoples perceptive and conversations full of assumptions can make you become a hero or a villain, I would like to think that I should be very careful and stay away from these people but then again I hardly see anyone these days so therefore I think I'm safe, I would like to think that I'm very lucky to be able to remove myself away from my misery even if it's momentarily or temporarily and also have the ability to be able to write my feelings and thoughts down on these pages, even though it doesn't make my miserable issues go away and it certainly doesn't solve any of my problems

Having that time out to write really does pump some fresh oxygen into my mental lungs that helps me to continue even though it gets uncontrollably rough and tough at times, I guess I'm only a human but without sounding negative or miserable I can only take so much.

I hope I don't run out of the fuel of life anytime soon. And for the rest of the day and night yes back to my coffees and cigarettes that are the only tools to help me through for the moment to see another day, I don't mention this to a lot of people simply because I am not in the mood to be patronizingly lectured by anyone.

February 17, 2020.

Apart from what happened and what not last night and early hours of this morning I've started my day quite and alone and enraged, at times if you look at my face you'll see the lights are on but nobody is home and at other times you look at my face and you'll see this scary, vicious and brutally savage animal that's frothing at the mouth with such a powerful anger and an insatiable hunger for blood with no considerations of any consequences.

I'm just in one of these moods today that nothing I mean nothing at all matters, today it's one of those days that I could easily end my life, I could easily end few peoples life's, I could end up in jail, nothing seems to matter and nothing has any value to me today, quite often I get this feeling that my mind is frozen with a strong sense of perplexity and at the same time nothing in my head is functioning at all, oh yes it does get very frightening I get the feeling of being more and more alone as if there's nobody left on this earth so there's no point in moving forward.

I do get in to these moods unwillingly quite often, the main problem with that is it seems to be very easy to find myself in these moods but trying to get out of it takes a long time in fact it can take up to six to eight hours before I can get some peace and relief, sometimes I wonder how long more will I keep on doing this, yeah just another unknown, and I'm always wandering with hope that next time I'm in one of these moods will I ever get out of it calmly and peacefully, again another unknown.

I know it's not an ideal way to live but as I mentioned before there's no tools available as yet, until such time comes where we have access to some useful tools that have been invented unfortunately it's a very fine line between staying or leaving, words are not good enough and assumptions based on other peoples experiences are definitely not useful tools and antidepressants are just another form of bandaid that can be quite detrimental to some peoples mental wellbeing.

Anyway, these are the unwanted and unneeded emotions I live with most days and yes I do wonder some days that how is it possible that I'm still here? Maybe I should thank my lucky stars, anyhow life goes on and it must, after all this is my life, my world and my problem nobody else's.

February 18, 2020.

Just another day today except a bit more confusing and I still haven't heard from Miss X yet to confirm what needs to happen about me going back to work, I have received an email from the insurer informing me that there are ten taxi vouchers have been confirmed for me to go to work and back and then not long after I get a phone call from the WI Dr telling me that I now have a non capacity form from the psychiatrist so there's no need for me to see her until after the fifth of March.

You probably getting confused reading this, anyway Miss X was supposed to be liaising with the insurer, WI Dr and the psychiatrist to constantly keep me informed but for some reason it's not happening swiftly, I'll just wait patiently until I hear from Miss X, yeah for someone that's so impatient and so eager to send me back to work with so little regard and no respect I am finding her to be unprofessional, lacking in her communicational abilities and very little maturity in general that can be easily intimidating, however in saying all that there's a sense of gladness in me that I am managing to keep a lid on my emotions, not losing my cool.

Okay, at eleven thirty am today I finally received a phone call from Miss X informing me that somehow she managed to convince the psychiatrist to overturn his decision to send me back to work on the twentieth of this month for three hours.

I agreed with her and told her that I will give it a go, no promises, but the fearful thought in my mind is not excluded that if anything goes wrong and something dreadful happens in my workplace that I end up behind bars or six foot under and that someone will get their hands on these pages and give Miss X and her company what they deserve, speaking strictly in legal terms, anyhow I did get in touch with the psychiatrist this afternoon, he explained to me briefly that his decision was not overturned and that if Miss X has any issues with that she can contact him directly and my non capacity form is valid until the fifth of March, so this obviously left me with a question mark that did Miss X gave me a verbal go ahead to go back to work against psychiatrist's written report of non capacity for employment? Hey today is not over yet, so I've called Miss X back and told her about my conversation with the psychiatrist and that she needs to call him and clear this mess and then let me know whether I'm going back to work or not.

She in return told me to call the psychiatrist back and ask him to change his mind, and to that I've asked her to get off the phone I am getting very angry and that I might say things to her that will be hurtful and offensive and then I hang up the phone, and so it's a waiting game again, I hope I don't run out of patience.

February 19, 2020.

With Miss X spending too much time on my radar lately has affected me so therefore I did have a terrible night last night with very limited sleep.

Yeah, still continuing with assorted pills and antidepressants, seen my family doctor this morning about my annual check up results and sure enough I've been told the same things like stop smoking and control my cholesterol.

Eleven thirty am at the moment I'm still waiting to hear from Miss X to get a confirmation whether I'm going back to work tomorrow or not, anyhow late this afternoon I did receive a call from Miss X telling me that she wasn't happy that she hasn't resolved this issue and she started to get a bit heavy with me telling me that I am not making enough effort to return to work, she came across like she has a personal vendetta against me, and then I firmly told her to pull her head in and explained to her that with the non capacity form in my hand there's no way I'm going back to work based on her verbal bull shit.

I mentioned to her that in the court of law her verbal bull shit has no validity and the non capacity form signed by the psychiatrist will stand much higher than her verbal instigations, so at the moment I feel that we don't have to revisit this confusion until after the fifth of March.

As I'm writing about this I can feel my anger levels are rising, I'm sweating, having breathing difficulties and my fists are firmly ready to jump into action mmmm no names, I just need to be silent again.

February 20, 2020.
Putting all my emotions, aches and pains aside this morning which I have spoken consecutively for so long I am getting sick and tired of mentioning the same things time and time again, so I meant to be back at work on light duties this morning for three hours to try and ease me into working environment, starting at nine thirty am, now it's almost midday I haven't heard from anyone yet, not that I was expecting it but it would have been a comforting thought and feeling that someone actually cares or thinking about me, not a chance hey!

This has been happening for the last eleven months now, I only hear from people if and when they need something or the useless people trying to get me back to work, it is ironic that to these people I am not important, it doesn't seem to matter what I'm feeling or how I'm feeling both mentally or physically, there's no respect and no compassion what so ever, it is really proven conformingly to me that I'm just a number, I am a nobody so this is how some of these so called professionals in their useless agenda can make you feel, now if you're still wandering where you can get some decent, genuine and useful help well good luck!

If I haven't mention it before well here it is you're on your own, if you're about to throw the towel in DON'T, you will be manipulated, you will be used and you will be taken advantage of, just to remember that every profession is an occupation and occupation equals to salary and dollars so at the end of the day you can answer your own question, what's more important? Your well being? Or the dollar signs, again I don't want to harshly criticize anyone and any of the professionals but this is how and what I feel right now

If I do come across a bit too heavy and offend some people well I do apologize, except Miss X with her unprofessionalism together with her rudeness doesn't stop there also with the people that put her in that position where she is not professionally conducting herself can really be heightening someone to a dangerous levels, anyway I can go on and on about all this, but if I'm not careful about all this negativity and toxicity that I can unwillingly inject some oxygen into the ability that can keep me on the tread mill of self destruction, so for now I will remove myself away from all this and put myself on another path where I can pursue some positive thoughts or try and remember some good memories, whichever comes first.

Well again you've guessed it right, for the rest of the day and night? yeah same old same old, I keep drumming it into my head that life goes on life goes on life goes on, I don't know why.

February 21, 2020.

Up and out of bed with some soreness in my left forearm all the way down to my wrist and some minor pain on the left shoulder, it was bearable but annoying, seen the physio this morning.

She worked mainly on my left forearm and stuck some needles on it as well and no work on the shoulder today, she told me that we'll pay more attention on and around the shoulder area next week, bit painful throughout the day and but bearable, still haven't heard from Miss X or anyone else that's on my case, nothing unusual I guess, however unless Miss X finds any other way of pushing me to go back to work I won't hear from her and that's sad.

Oh well, I'm used to all this incompetence, inconsideration and being just another number,

February 24, 2020.

I didn't write about anything the last two days but that doesn't mean that my mind takes a break or my aches and pains gives me any relief at all, I just didn't want to write about my anguish, yeah it does get to a point where I'm sick and tired of all this and sometimes I ask myself what's the point of writing about all of this?

For a while there my mind stops, every think becomes blank, sitting out in the backyard on my own with my coffees and cigarettes it really does take a long time to get some functionality back in my thoughts and then I start to think again, thinking that someday someone reading this book might have some similarities of what I'm going through that if or when I get out of this with the completion of this book might be helpful for someone else to pull through as well, one would always hope, anyhow seen the psychologist this morning and she was concerned about my attitude today, she told me that about two weeks ago I was starting to get better, however this morning she was worried and concerned with the signs of anger I have been displaying without realizing.

She insisted that I let her know so that she can help me in some way, and when I've explained last week's poor handling of my return to work program by Miss X, the insurer, the psychiatrist and my employer made me very angry and it all reactivated some bad and negative thoughts in my head, especially with Miss X's misconduct and how dangerously close it was almost losing it with her, so after letting the psychologist know she gave me some lecture and some home work that when I get home I should go on line do some meditation to try and calm myself down.

Once again I tried to tell her that meditation doesn't work for me, my concentration and tolerance levels are way down but in saying all that I've assured her that I'm not dangerous in any way at the moment and that if Miss X has anything coming to her in any way, shape or form it won't be from me, so the rest of the day I will be getting myself ready for tomorrow's meeting with my lawyer, anxiously waiting to see what the outcome will be, as I keep saying there's a lot of unknown for the future.

I have no idea where I'm going to end up or what's going to happen, but one thing for sure is that I'm so tired and so fed up with all this, I just want it all to end one way or another.

February 25, 2020.

Got up and out of bed this morning feeling a bit more anguish, more nervous, more anxious a lot more heavy breathing, maybe it's because I have an appointment with my lawyer this morning.

It's to see if I'm entitled to a common law claim and what happens with my bullying and harassment claim, so nine am this morning we're in the lawyer's office with my wife, and the young lawyer explained to us that I'm entitled to some common law claim for pain and suffering and that we have a good case for bullying and harassmen.

In hearing that from my lawyer I didn't care much about the dollar value but to have someone accountable for me being bullied and harassed was a lot more important to me, much more than money, so the lawyer carefully explained it to me and my wife that the firm has appointed a barrister and that I will need to give a clear and honest statement under oath and that we will go to court so that I can get some closure for my mental pain and suffering.

The young lawyer was very thorough and she prepared me for the barrister and also for my employers lawyers that they may blame me for my injuries and that I might have contributed to my injuries on the grounds of my own negligence, well not only having two surgeries one on my left shoulder and one on my left forearm and physical pain and suffering and on top of that with bullying and harassment causing me mental pain and suffering as well and on top of all that my employers lawyers will try and put all the blame on me as if I've contributed to my injuries was a bit over the top.

Anyhow, having so much confidence in my lawyer and putting my trust in her capable hands my wife and I left her office without me showing any emotions or losing my cool, but in saying all that though when I arrived home I almost collapsed in the back yard deep in my thoughts, thinking that from the beginning of all this physical and mental pain and suffering for the last eleven months that my employers lawyer's are going to make me feel like a villain and make me feel like I've brought all this pain and suffering up on myself, wow!!

Talking about self esteem, self confidence and talking about being treated like just another number, what a great confirmation, well these are more professionals that f$%^s with my head so how the hell am I supposed to heal and recover? When this kind of stuff happens time and time again, you see I find it very easy to write about all this rather than talking to anyone.

Somehow and in some way I would get to be labelled a sook or a whinger, so there you go I can't win, so the meeting with my lawyer today confirms to me that there are still a lot of stormy days and rocky roads ahead, so be it. It's been absolute hell in the last eleven months trying to make everyone that's involved in my case to believe and understand me that what I feel and what I'm going through is f$%^ing real, it surely has been an uphill battle and still continuing.

I am praying, hoping and wishing that I'll get better and all this will go away and my life will get back to some normality again, amongst all this going on in my head I've received a call from Miss X, it was as per f#$%ing usual, it was all about me returning to work, well I think my hyper verbal vocabulary got the better of me that the phone conversation with her did not end well with me swearing and losing my cool.

Not long after the conversation with Miss X I received a call from one of the case managers from the insurer trying to entice me to go back to work by telling me that if I do go back to work soon there will be a bonus for me and that I will be getting more money in my pay packet, wow, wow, and wow more incompetent professional that I'm dealing with.

Anyhow, I politely told him what he can do with his bonus and that I'm not interested in more money and that I just need to recover and get back to normal, so we finished the conversation by him telling me that he will organize a meeting between myself and the insurers psychiatrist at a later date, and I did tell him yes okay and that I have nothing to hide.

February 26, 2020.
Up and out of bed very early again this morning, as much as I don't want to talk or write about my issues hour by hour everyday but I feel everything minute by minute, because I don't talk to anyone anymore so I feel the need to at least write about it, and when I do get out of bed every morning this is how my day starts.

Thinking about the antidepressants that have no effectiveness, thinking about the sleeping pills that are not working and the pain killers that only work for an hour or two.

I know thinking about these with coffees and cigarettes early in the morning is not a great way to start the day but none of this is within my reach to control, anyway I've visited my mum mid morning today, it was great again that's where I get a bit of peace and serenity, I wish I could do it more often, you probably asking why don't I ? well even that short two to three hours in my mum's presence just like I do at home I put on a false smile pretend that everything is okay so mum will have no reason to worry about me,.

as soon as I arrived home I received a call from a different case manager from the insurer telling me how important it is for me to go back to work and how important it is for my mental wellbeing and that she will organize a psychiatrist from her department together with her and myself in her office.

I told her that it would be okay just let me know where and when, oh by the way this lady didn't even ask me if I was okay both mentally or physically, when our conversation ended I thought about it for a while, now little while ago I've signed a consent form with each of the medical professional including the insurer that they can exchange any information about me, now why would the insurer want me to go into their office to find out what? When they can easily get in touch with the psychiatrist and the psychologist I am currently seeing.

I thought I should get a legal advice about this so I've called my lawyer, she told me to give her five minutes she will call the insurer and then get back to me.

She did and she told me not to worry about any of these and that I will be left alone until the eleventh of March, so in a nut shell the insurer and Miss X are doing everything they can to end my case and get me off their records, so yes this is a constant reminder that I am just another number where I get no respect, no compassion and no care factor.

There are not many options but to keep going, except some drastic options that I really don't want go onto right now, I am doing okay for the moment not to let the pilot light ignite anything

It does become a very fine line between holding on and letting go, the pressure is very heavy and very real, I would like to keep on thinking that weakness is not an option I guess I need to keep on using all my strength wisely as long as I can and where I can.

February 27, 2020.
When I walked outside into the backyard early this morning with my ever reliable tools of coffees and cigarettes I found myself feeling empty, nothing on the agenda, nothing to focus on and to be honest no care factor for anything.

I just want to have a manageable day with no negativities at all and the way I'm feeling now I don't even care about any positivity's at all, anyway about midday I've checked my emails and to my surprise I have one email from my zero favourite person Miss X asking me if she can attend my session with my psychiatrist, wow what a pit bull I thought, she sunk her teeth into me she won't let go, but she doesn't realize that her hungry eagerness for a reward can really damage a person like me and push me to go all the way to the point of no return.

Anyhow, I replied by saying that I would preferred to see the psychiatrist on my own, so for now I'll just be waiting to hear from her to see what else has she manifested.

You see dealing with all this bull shit on daily basis in my current situation is really damaging my ability to concentrate on my mental recovery, being faced with all this regularly makes my mind wander off in different directions, here's one of the directions that I constantly think about these days is that my mind feels so contaminated with all these anger, resentment, hatred and regret issues that it will take a long long time to flush it all out of my head but I'm not sure if I will ever get the chance to flush it all out before my time ends on this earth.

I don't know if I'm ever going to regain some kind of normality some kind of happiness again or will I reach my destination ending my journey in a miserable state.

Why I feel and think like this is because of the four emotions I've mentioned above the anger, the resentment, the hatred and the regrets become the elements of ankle and wrist bracelets, two of these emotions are on my ankles and two of them are on my wrists with chains keeping me tied down in my darkness, not only feeling like a caged animal but being tied down with these emotions leaves me powerless, making me except that there's no way out of this, and at this darkest hour or the darkest minute of my existence I keep wandering what sort of tools or help be made available to deter me away from using my last option to get me out of my misery, it is a frightening thought it is a very scary thought that using the last option can be made very easy by being constantly bombarded with unnecessary opprobrium from inexperienced and useless people that don't know how damaging their actions can be, and at the very last minute of actioning any ideation and going through with it doesn't make you a bad person it doesn't make you an idiot or stupid and not actioning any ideation doesn't make you a hero or a survivor so you really can't brag.

Not actioning any ideations can really leave you feeling ashamed that you've contemplated the idea and embarrassed that you almost went all the way with it but then again on the other hand do you feel embarrassed and ashamed that you didn't action it, you weren't strong enough? You felt weak?

So all this leaves us with so many questions as to why it was done and why it wasn't done and all these questions will remain unanswered maybe forever, I live with these questions on daily basis, and quite often just like now I can't control the tears rolling down my face but hey the field will always be open for assumptions, guessing and investigations, the investigation will be rolled into an assumption and then the assumption will become an artificial information that will be turned into knowledge that will be given to professionals to be used on patients.

Unfortunately, we will never know the real reasons. And further more when I didn't go through with my own ideations even today I still don't know if I've failed or what was the real reason that I've changed my mind to stick around a little longer.

I know that feeling of almost letting go is always with me that I can't let go of and it scares me that it will always be with me, it is a daunting thought that it can reignite at anytime, I truly hope to find the real reason why I didn't go through with the two attempts, and if I do find the reasons anytime soon I will surely put it on these pages.

February 28, 2020.
Seen the physio this morning, she was concerned that both my shoulder and my left forearm was in pain and both had limited movements, so she will write a letter to the surgeon to see what can be done, maybe stronger pain killers or whatever else.

Well, I'll be seeing the surgeon on the fourth of March, received a call from one of the officials of the insurer today asking me if she and a mental health specialist from her office can attend my next session with me and the psychiatrist on the fifth of March, here we go again more mental disturbance.

The question constantly remains on how the hell can I recover? So I did tell her that her and whoever she wants can go and see my psychiatrist whenever they like but not in my presence, so she said she will call the psychiatrist and then call me back to let me know what the outcome is.

My lawyer called about midday assuring me that everything is in order for us to go to court so that there's some accountability and at the end of all this some closure, anyway the report I've received from the physio this morning about the constant pain on my forearm and that it's a very slow progress.

I've emailed it to the insurer, my lawyer and to Miss X, it's about three thirty now I'm not sure if I'm going to hear from anyone at stage. I'm coming to terms with the idea that the case manager from the insurer and Miss X are totally careless and they have no knowledge what so ever of the damage they are causing, I am very angry with the way they are pushing me to go back to work, my only fear at the moment is I will lose control, I truly don't want to put anyone's safety at risk, so this is just another day where I have skin full of shit that I will see the rest of the day and night through in my miserable and agoraphobic state, I think it's best for everyone that I stay out of sight.

February 29, 2020.
Three forty am at the moment I've been up for about an hour or so, yes with my usual tools of contentment my coffees and cigarettes, thinking about the beginning and the end of my day today but

for some strange reason I can feel it's going to be another useless, pointless and fruitless day again.

Naturally thinking like this already directly or indirectly opens up a lot of grounds in my mind to entertain some different ideas of revenge that's obviously driven by anger that activates the rage, followed by shortness of breath, sweat and tears, it hurts to think that I have no option but to keep calm.

My Obligations and the consequences of what I might be capable of are the major debilitating factors on my path that I cannot action some of these serious fundamentals of sweet revenge, this is not the first time and it won't be the last time that I keep on thinking like this and I don't need to elaborate on this any further, and among all these thoughts I'm still searching for the genuine reasons as to why am I able to keep calm and how is it that I am still keeping the lid on some dangerous activities.

I hope one day I will maybe not all but some answers to some of these serious questions, anyhow for the rest of the day and night just the usual stuff with lots of mixed emotions that extracts a lot of my reserved strength and energy for no valuable outcome at all, dead minutes, dead hours, dead days and dead weeks and so on, it's a one way journey with no vision, one day I hope to find the comforting thought as to why this is all worth it.

March 1, 2020.

Just a usual again, out of bed early this morning and into the backyard in the dark, spend considerable amount of time outside feeling sentimental about the two darkest days of my life in twenty nineteen.

I have already revealed some details of April nineteenth of twenty nineteen but I'm not ready to talk about October twelfth twenty nineteen, maybe one day soon when I gain enough courage and confidence I might be able to write about it, today is not the day, today I just want a reliable and trusted hand on my shoulder telling me that everything is going to be alright, it looks like I'll be waiting for that hand for a long time.

Anyway, I constantly keep on praying that I can keep the lid on a little longer, I truly don't want myself in a situation full of regrets, all I hope and wish for right now is god to give me more patience and more strength to keep on dealing with what I have at the moment, and it's not easy and I know for a fact that it can't be understood by just anyone. It's hard and it's real.

March 2, 2020.
Seen the psychologist this morning, there were a couple of concerns from her, she has seen some anger in me and she was concerned about the pain on my left shoulder and especially the pain on my left forearm.

My anger is mainly related to Miss X and the case manager from the insurer that they are observing and trying to manipulate every avenue to get me back to work without any consideration of my wellbeing in any shape or form.

The psychologist told me that she understands how this is disturbing me deeply and that she will contact Miss X and the case manager to have a discussion with them both, and she assured me that she will contact my physio and have a discussion with her about some pain management, we'll see how it all turns out, so in the mean while everything is as usual as it has been in the last eleven months, I just don't want to write anymore, I simply don't want to repeat about anything again and again.

I am just so sick and truly tired of all this bullshit, I just want it all to end now so I can get on with my life, it almost feels like I'm running out of patience and time, yeah it is hurtfully worrying.

March 3, 2020.
I think the issue about sleepless nights is that maybe I need to put all my emotions to one side and try to forget about them temporarily so I might be able to get some solid sleep that's more than just an hour.

Now days when I do get out of bed it takes me about two to three hours to bring the pain on my left shoulder especially the left forearm down to a manageable level with pain killers, the pain killers ease the pain but the pain is not eliminated completely, that's another issue on day to day basis.

I have noticed it that people don't want to hear about it and they don't want to know about my aches and pains, that shouldn't be the case but I'm learning to live with it, good thing that I'm seeing the surgeon tomorrow where I can get useful information and assistance on what to do about the pain on my left forearm. It's four am at the moment so I guess I'll be pushing shit uphill for the rest of the day and night.

I am still very thankful that I'm able to write my thoughts down on these pages, if I was able to talk to people on mutual grounds with mutual respect I probably wouldn't be writing anything, anyway here's something positive I am starting to reduce the number of cigarettes from sixty per day to about forty five but the number of coffees are still the same, the number can escalate up to twelve coffees on some days.

As I mentioned before there are worst habits I can procure, anyway while another day is disappearing in me being in a useless state and almost waiting for one of my treaters there are on my case to call me or email me with some disturbing proposal or disturbing news to ruin my day and night even more, so the inevitable just like any other day has happened, received an email from Miss X at two pm today, again with no concern and no respect informing me that she has put together a return to work program for me, firstly I'm trying very hard not to let this get to a boiling point in my head, now I think I have every right and reason to be angry with this vindictively avenging lady that's trying to send me back to work without clearances from the psychiatrist, psychologist, surgeon and the work injury doctor.

I still don't understand why is this vindictive, inexperienced and disrespectful lady (Miss X) is still on my case, you probably wandering if I have reported her yes I have and each time I get told that someone will have a word with her, after having a short discussion with my lawyer she told me to ignore it and let it go and if and when my treaters give me the go ahead about me going back to work then I'll start regaining my employment prospect and keeping it alive as long as it takes.

Wow, that sounds promising it sounds great it sounds positive, oh yeah as long as I pick myself up off the bottom and out of my darkness and get some kind of control over my emotions that's if there are positive tools available, then yes my future employment prospects can be achievable, wouldn't that be great.

March 4, 2020.

Today I don't want to talk about how my night was, how long I slept or didn't sleep or how much pain I was in and how many pills I consumed including antidepressants.

As much as I find it annoyingly boring writing about it all the time I'm sure by now you've had enough of reading about it all, I've seen the surgeon this morning about my left forearm, before I attended my appointment I've prepared myself with few questions like what's the time frame for complete recovery, why does the bone in my left forearm feels like it's bruised, do I need pain killers temporarily or permanently and why does the pain shoot up to ten out of ten when I make certain moves with my left forearm?

So the surgeon informed me that it will take six months or more to recover and there's no certainty for a full one hundred percent recovery so therefore he gave me a referral to see a hand therapist in one of the western suburbs of Melbourne and he also gave me a non capacity form until the first of April.

So here I go again I need to inform the insurer to get an approval to make an appointment with the hand therapist, to get an approval from the insurer and make an appointment to see the hand therapist could take weeks, so there's my point again it doesn't seem to matter how much pain I'm in and how many pain killers I will have to consume before I see the hand therapist well okay I did inform the case manager from the insurer and I also informed Miss X.

For now I will wait and see what happens and how long it takes to get any reply from the insurer and Miss X .

March 5 2020.
Seen the psychiatrist this morning, we had a longer chat today then we normally do, he showed some signs of concern with my mental and physical pain so that he was reluctant to give me any forms today.

    I think he will be communicating with Miss X, the case manager and WI Dr via email or on the phone, he also told me not to drive a manual car for a while, anyway I can't remember anything else from today's session with the psychiatrist, the communications I have with any of the treaters unless it's written down or I get it emailed to me I simply can't remember more than eighty percent of it. Anyhow having a restless and unsettled day again.

    I have a non capacity form until the first of April so I've asked Miss X do we still see the WI Dr next week? Her reply was Yes and that we need to meet to discuss my treatment plan and recommendations for returning to work, wow again, I know I shouldn't but I need to write down exactly how I feel this minute.

    I would like to think that I'm not a bad person to wish any harm on anyone, one thing with someone like Miss X is that she is blindly so dedicated to her job that she is forgetting the meaning of compassion, respect and caring.

    I think the only way she's ever going to understand these values is that if someone she dearly loves is diagnosed with some life threatening illness maybe then she will show some kindness and respect to the people around her, I know it might be terrible for me to think like this, but I am openly and honestly writing down exactly what I'm feeling in these moments. I don't wish no harm on anyone that don't deserve it, but the ones I constantly contemplate on inflicting physical pain is another story.

March 6, 2020.
Seen the physio this morning, not much in the way of exercise due to limited movement and excessive pain on my left forearm, she showed me some light movements for me to do at home until next Friday and I assured her that I will do my best.

It's eleven forty five pm at the moment not much else today, just stewing in my own misery without bothering anyone and trying to keep my anger issues under control, That's it!.

March 8 2020.
Two forty five am now and I'm already outside with my coffee and cigarettes, great way to start a brand new day, yesterday was a quiet day not much to write about except just thinking about the shit storm I receive from Miss X and the case manager from the insurer on regular basis that I'm so over it.

Anyway, I am getting used to the idea of spending my days and nights mostly alone where I don't speak to anyone to reignite anything in my head or to relive any of the unpleasant experiences, just waiting for the day where if and when I am fully recovered I can get to appreciate the good people that's been with me by my side all along and totally disregard the fake friends and some family members.

As you can see with a lot of these negative thoughts going around and around in my head constantly that it's extremely hard to see the bright side of life if there is brighter side to life, some days like today it becomes very very hard to find a good reason for deterrence, at times like today as much as I may think that there's no point in going forward, but at the same time I think of the reasons why I should stay around a little longer, whether the reasons are good or not I do find it hard to differentiate.

March 9 2020.
Four thirty am now I've been sitting outside already had three cups of coffees and I'm sure there will be a few more to come.

Sitting outside in the darkness in the early hours of the morning felt the same as the darkness I've been living almost a year now, it actually made me think for a while that just like the sun will up in three to four hours there will be light and that everything will be visible, so I thought of the same about my darkness that I will come out of it someday that with some light shinning everything in my head will be clear and visible.

I guess thinking like this can only give me some hope that I don't let go, I don't give up and most importantly I don't give in to all the negativities in my head and I also understand and except that giving in can positively mean the end.

I would still find someone on a similar situation as I am, I know it won't fix anything and I know I won't achieve anything but it would be comforting to know that I'm not alone, as I've always founded hard to talk to anyone.

I wish I could find someone that understands how one day you can fly like an eagle so high, so confident, so dignified and next you're like a sparrow with broken wings and it takes such a long time to fly like an eagle again, so when I sit outside looking into emptiness drinking lots of coffees and having countless cigarettes all these things and lots and lots more always goes through my head.

I just can't help it I guess, but for the moment I wish I had maximum confidence that soon my sun will rise and shine so I will see and understand a lot of things clearly, I can only hope.

Chapter 20

March 11, 2020.
Seen the work injury Doctor (WI Dr) together with Miss X, when we started our conference/consultation it quickly become clear to both of them that I wasn't ready mentally or physically to go back to work or even talk about work until the eighth of April.

The Doctor suggested that I should talk to my physio about aqua therapy and if it's okay to get a referral so the insurer can approve it, and then I've explained my anger situation to both of them in a good and extended level, they were both concerned about what I've explained and towards the end of the consultation I was asked if I had any questions, well I thought this is good, and I started by facing Miss X and saying not a question but a request and asked her if she can start showing me some respect and every now and then just ask me how am I feeling and if I'm okay.

At first she was a bit startled then she quickly recovered and assured me the that she will comply, the look in her face gave me the impression that my request was understood and excepted, I think I will keep this up as long as it takes with people like Miss X so that I don't damage anything in and around my house like I did last month, just because I'm down and just about out doesn't mean that I shouldn't get the respect I deserve. Again I don't feel the need to write down about the rest of the day and night as it happens to be the same old same old.

March 12, 2020.
When I got out of bed early this morning there was a pleasant easiness in the pain on my left forearm, early this month when I've

seen the surgeon I've explained the pain on my left arm being eight out of ten after the surgery, so he prescribed some anti inflammatory tablets that I've been taken, maybe they starting to effectively work on my arm that the pain is right down to between one and two out of ten.

If I make certain moves that it can escalate up to nine out of ten. Overall if I can control and reduce the unnecessary moves with my left arm therefore the pain becomes manageable.

With so much reduced physical pain can obviously and inevitably allow me to start working on my mental issues, and start managing my anger and the real issues that ignites my anger, with all these issues I'm dealing with I know I'm not silly, I'm not stupid and I'm not an idiot, I have realized that I am a man that fallen into darkness a bit too deep and in a constant struggle to get out of it. With my mind constantly being occupied with lots of negative issues that it's almost impossible to allow some positivity in my head or in my heart.

I can't handle hearing the phrase " time and patience" well time doesn't heal anything it just passes by and patience well we can run out of very quickly, so yes it's just a useless phrase that is used on people who are in doubt to amuse them, there's no reality in it. Yeah it is a big statement I know and I can confidently say that it's not working on me at the moment.

March 13, 2020.

Seen the physio this morning, after working on my left shoulder and the forearm she assured me that she will contact the insurer to get me an approval for hydrotherapy at a local leisure centre, she told me that the approval can take up to three weeks and once we get it the treatment can take up to four months, well I am very hopeful and optimistic about this, I'll try anything to make it work so that I can get the full usage of my left shoulder and forearm.

As I'm writing about all this I'm already thinking about Monday morning that I'll be seeing the psychologist and she'll be questioning me about the last two weeks of what happened, how I felt and what I thought of and so on, this happens with the psychiatrist and with the WI Dr, now having a full on conversation with these people on a regular basis can be good or bad, the good part is that talking to these people about what's happened today and the last couple of days is okay but the bad thing is when we start talking about suicide ideations or harming others over and over again can and really does make it extremely hard to keep the lid on firmly, if I wanted to completely forget about what could have happened and never wanted to revisited.

It becomes almost impossible not to relive it again and again, and while I'm trying to deal this unwarranted ordeal on every hour of the day I'm still dealing with disrespectful Miss X regularly about her pushing me to go back to work regardless of the circumstances and maybe even consequences, oh yeah it does become extremely frustrating that these people don't hear me, they don't listen to me and when they look in my direction they don't see me.

I really am so over all this, I just want to get better as soon as possible, I would dearly love to put all this behind me and get on with my life as normal as possible, just because I haven't been writing much about my mental situation lately doesn't mean that I'm out of the woods, oh no far from it, I still have lots and lots of deep and dark moments where some invisible powers dictates me to spend most of my time alone.

One day if and when this ordeal is over it'll be great to be out of the darkness where in some positive light I can lick my wounds and get to stand on my own two feet positively and confidently again. Yeah it's a good thing I get to write all my thoughts and my feelings on these pages in my own space in my house where it feels like a sacred place that I can do it twenty four seven as long as I'm not disturbed, I do realize and except that I do not wish to become a high risk or hazardous to anyone and I don't want anyone to feel unsafe around me, I'm saying this is because I've had days and sometimes still do have very little concerns about other people's safety around me.

I have gone through days where I didn't care for anyone or anything, it didn't matter if it was a life or death situation, the ideation of self harm or harming others is never on a normal level, it always fluctuates from a high risk, low risk or no risk quite swiftly, it's not easy always living with the fear of it igniting at any minute, I think this is the part that is misunderstood by many people, it really is a very complex issue.

Since I've been in this situation I have communicated with some people on and off the social media and I found that no one has any answers, it can be confusing that we cannot differentiate between breakdown, anxiety, depression or any other mental health issues, what I'm trying to say in my humble opinion is that whenever a mental health professional speaks to me I have this rejective resistance to believe that they have any confirmed knowledge, what I tend to understand and believe that it is only highly statistically gathered useless assumptions that can really drive you up the wall.

Unfortunately until there's solid evidence of confirmed tools to help us get out of the situation we're in there will be lots of innocent lives lost, I do apologize for having such a powerful and critical opinion about this but this is how I feel and what I feel at the moment. Besides there are twenty four hours in a day where most of these hours are occupied with lots and lots of these thoughts, yeah mostly negative not much positive, I except just can't help it.

March 16, 2020.

Seen the psychologist this morning, with the generosity of the insurer I went there and back with a taxi, I still can't drive my own vehicle yet, not long to go before I can drive I hope, well with the psychologist it was inevitable again, touched base on some of the stuff that might have been unwanted or un approved by me, but with me placing my trust in her thinking that she might be doing her best to help me to get rid of my misery so therefore I go along willingly with whatever the instructions she throws at me.

I can't help but to think that all these sessions are embellishing the truth to build my ego but on the other hand it can be devastatingly hurtful and disappointing to give me false hope by being told that everything is going to be alright.

However I am starting to develop an ability to be able to see and understand that my recovery and wellbeing might entirely be up to me to instigate where ever and whenever possible, but as I've been saying all along if the right tools were available it could be achievable, then again without being overly critical the tools might be right on my path where I'm failing to see, who knows one day soon someone might have the ability to point them out to me for me to use them tools appropriately, anyway the rest of the day and night predominantly the same thoughts and feelings of never ending anguish.

It doesn't seem to matter how much I try to brainwash myself that everything is going to be alright and that all this will be over soon, but there's no avail, even though I keep revisiting this thought over and over again with no avail I am trying to be cautious and be very alert that it doesn't bring me to the brink of giving up altogether for good.

March 17, 2020.

My wife and I have seen the lawyer this morning, the reason my wife came along is that I still can't drive, so the lawyer made me sign some forms.

ne of them was the common law claim for pain and suffering and she assured me that everything was fine and everything was on track for us to go to court about me being bullied and harassed at my work place that this will be acknowledged and I will get a closure once and for all.

When I arrived home I've emailed the case manager of the insurer about an approval to see the hand therapist which I've been waiting since the fourth of March, yeah it leaves a question mark on my mind that the insurer and Miss X are vigorously pushing me to go back to work without any consideration, yet when it comes to medical treatment approvals it can take weeks if not months, contradiction of terms one would believe, as long as I go back to work it really doesn't seem to matter how I feel or what I feel.

Anyhow, that's life maybe at times we may think that there's so much to take in, maybe not, maybe it's the way some people try so aggressively and vigorously to get their message across that gets on peoples nerves, maybe that's when we lose control and get angry to the point where it's much higher than the initial issue is worth, but at that point of anger and relentlessness it becomes extremely hard to calm down to identify what's right or wrong, this is when my own tools of coffees and cigarettes comes very handy.

I sometimes wish that I had shares in coffee and cigarette companies that I can see a small fortune developing, if not for me at least for my wife and my children where they can benefit from it whether I'm here or not.

March 20, 2020.

Seen the physio this morning, mild exercise on left shoulder and left forearm and she assured me that she will organize the appropriate forms together with the insurer for me to attend hydrotherapy treatment at a local leisure centre as soon as possible.

Not long after I've seen the psychologist usual conversations however she told me that she had a long discussion with someone from the insurer which happens to be a psychiatrist, apparently there were a lot of questions asked about me and my psychologist told me that she will have further discussions with the lady from the insurer this afternoon, whatever the outcome of their conversations, I'm sure I won't be informed but that's how it goes.

Anyhow, I've explained my situation to my psychologist that all I need right now is an approval from the insurer to see the hand therapist, I am still waiting since the fourth of this month, I don't know and I'm not sure why it takes so long to get an approval from the insurer, I've had the same problem leading up to my left shoulder surgery and six months later the same issue with my left forearm surgery.

Sometimes I question myself about my patience levels, I know for a fact sometimes my patience levels go very low on the scale. I guess with the acceptance of being just another number in the corporate world you get to except the unexplainable and unacceptable delays without a choice, however if this was a private matter and I had private insurance a lot of these medical issues would have been solved within days. But that's life not just this but with a lot of other corporate issues we just go along with it.

March 27, 2020.
Seen the physio this morning, due to uncertainty of corona virus and having to wear a mask I didn't feel comfortable being there, so therefore no exercise took place, we had a bit of a chat about home exercise and made a new appointment for the seventeenth of April

We also spoke about hydrotherapy that was approved by the insurer but I didn't think it was a good idea with the current corona virus pandemic so I will decline until it's safe for me to attend. Anyway it's day twenty three and I'm still waiting for an approval to see the hand therapist, I'm still not sure why the insurer are taking their time, my forearm is not healing well and it is painful, I do have a referral from the surgeon but I can't do much about it just got to wait until I get the approval.

I didn't write anything the last six days, I wasn't in a right state of mind, both physically and mentally I feel tired I feel drained and getting very frustrated, well with the current covid nineteen isolation which doesn't mean anything to me because I've been isolating since March last year in my own little environment, so the main factor at the moment is the pain on my left forearm has been going up and down based on the effects of the pain killers I'm currently taking, because of the limited usage of my forearm I find this effects the healing of my left shoulder in a desirable time frame, so therefore left shoulder and forearm combined gives me a lot of grief.

This obviously plays on my mind somewhat positively and negatively constantly, thinking that I will be suffering with this pain for the rest of my life, constantly thinking like this can only direct me towards lots of negative thoughts, so it's quite natural that I get upset and that creates a lot of anger issues, little things bother me, people in general bother me, my kids bother me, some of my treaters bother me worse of all my wife bothers me for no reason at all and definitely no fault of hers at all.

I just haven't been able to tolerate with anything and anybody lately, so yeah my anger much much higher that makes me want to destroy things and certain people, and at times I find it extremely hard to refrain myself, so that's one of the reasons why I find it safe for me and for some people that I spend a lot of my days and nights at home. The main safety for me is late at night and mostly past midnight with very little sleep and than from approximately three or four in the morning with my coffees and cigarettes watching the beginning of a brand new day, this happens quite a lot one thing about this though I get tired during day and it feels safer for me not to damage anything and I can't do anything to anyone that I might end up with regrets.

This goes on day after day while I'm putting up with the pain on my forearm and my shoulder and the numbness on the left hand with occasional pins and needles. Anyway about the dark place I'm still in which I truly don't want to talk about at the moment simply because I've excepted that there's no help no solution only words and assumptions so forget it! So if I can I need to help myself, Maybe one day.

April 1, 2020.
Got up this morning about three thirty am with heavy numbness on my left hand, it became a bit scary that it took me about twenty minutes of rubbing the left hand that I started to panic.

After a little while I rushed outside with my coffee and cigarettes to watch the beginning of another brand new day, getting ready for another useless, pointless and hopeless day ahead and not to mention certain degree of pain on my left shoulder and arm.

I found that I have already been isolating for the last twelve months with physical pain and mental issues and now with this corona virus restrictions and isolations being in the house twenty four seven with my wife.

I haven't been associating with anyone the last twelve months so for me it's nothing new but as for my wife with these new restrictions means that she spends more time at home with me so I feel sorry for her, with my mental state and my anger issues that I am trying my hardest to keep it all under control, I'm trying not to show any of it to my wife, it is driving me up the wall.

I am finding myself picking faults in just about anything and everything, it's not good not good at all. Anyhow had a phone consultation with the forearm surgeon this morning, he told me that he hasn't heard from the insurer about hand therapist approval that I've been waiting since fourth of March and that he will contact the case manager himself to highlight the urgency as to why I need an approval to see the hand therapist, we'll see what happens and how long it takes, so for me to sit back and wait patiently and at the same time try and try to keep calm as much as I can.

April 6, 2020.
Up early this morning again nothing new nothing different I thought until I've checked my emails and to my surprise I received one from the case manager last Friday informing me that I have the approval to see the hand therapist, the reason for me to find this out this morning is that I haven't paid much attention to anything the last few days again.

I do go through some hours during the day where I'm completely oblivious to anything around me, motionless and lots of blank moments, so when I did regain some momentum I've called the hand therapist and made an appointment for Thursday at four pm, and with the hand therapist I'm not sure if it's going to delay my recovery process, I guess I'll just wait patiently to see what happens and how long it will take.

Anyhow, sitting here thinking and writing about all these the tears are rolling down my face again trying not to have this feeling of abdication and trying not to reject the idea that things might turn out alright, somehow someday I will need to find the way to stop being a despondent person.

In order to get out of this angst I need to start manifesting some positive and happy thoughts without antidepressants, hoping to find out that this could be within my capability, however I still don't believe in the saying that " time heals everything" no it doesn't, the only way the healing could be achieved is if I instigate and contribute time and effort towards the healing process, yeah well I'll need to leave this manifestation for another day, today is not the day.

April 8, 2020.
Had a phone consultation with the WI Dr this morning, due to corona virus restrictions I couldn't go to the clinic.

The Doctor has given me a non capacity for work form until the sixth of May and told me that we will wait and see the outcome of the hand therapist's treatment for us to determine the next move.

Apart from the consultation this morning nothing new and not much else is happening and with this corona virus restrictions I feel more isolated, just got to keep riding the waves and making sure that I don't crash.

Here's another new thought that's been bothering me recently that I'm starting to blame myself for all that's been happening in the last twelve months, well for instance we can create our own misery by making wrong and bad choices and contribute more and more to our misery by having negative, sad and dangerous thoughts to the point where our head feels like it's going to explode, this is where I'm finding it hard to understand and except that I did not contribute to my accident at work almost six years ago and I don't believe I contributed to the change of attitude in people that I worked with for almost twelve years.

I hope one day I'm lucky enough to find out and understand why and how peoples attitude can change ever so unashamedly, so yeah I can't help wandering was it a wrong choice working with this company? Was it a bad choice associating with the people I've worked with? And will I ever allow this to happen again?

So there you have it this goes on and on almost endlessly. Anyway the rest of the day and night will be the same with my ever so faithful tools of coffees and cigarettes to see another day through without it being exasperated.

April 9, 2020.
Seen the hand therapist this afternoon on the west side of Melbourne for the first time, I found him to be a real professional, he put my left wrist and forearm in a splint for up to eight weeks to stabilize the movement of my left hand so that my forearm can heal quicker, I was happy with his attitude and his professionalism, I will see

him again on the twentieth of this month to see how my forearm is healing. I just wish I could find a mental professional like the hand therapist that knows exactly how to get into my head, work with it, fix it and improve it so I can get back to living a normal life again.

Then I can stop pretending that everything is alright, especially in the presence of my wife it is extremely hard for me to show her that I'm okay.

April 13, 2020.
Another useless and senseless night and all day today, hearing on the news and talking about corona virus and how annoying it is that we're all self isolating.

I wouldn't try and tell people that I've been self isolating for the last twelve months, but hey that's my problem, anyway I really don't give a rats arse about the corona virus outbreak, I think it is a manifestly fabricated outbreak that may have monetary benefits and gains for some reputable organisations that we will never know

I think as a nation we don't like to be kept in the dark and knowing that we will never be told the truth, and in the general public this will all be theoretical and speculative assumption for years to come.

April 15, 2020.
Seen the psychiatrist today, well fruitless as usual and it is starting to feel like a conventional procedure that's been put together by insurers, employers and approved by some government body to become a bureaucratic red tape that I keep on seeing the psychiatrist on regular basis.

The main question I was asked by the psychiatrist today is that Do I need more antidepressants?

Well the rest of the day and night has been blank and pointless thoughts with no resolution in sight, being on this unknown journey without knowing which direction I am travelling does become unbearable most times but that's life, I just need to wait and see where and when this all ends.

April 17, 2020.

I've cancelled my physio appointment for this morning for two reasons, corona virus and the splint on my forearm, next time I see the hand therapist I will ask him if I can still attend my physio sessions providing that I take off the splint during exercising and put it back on at the end of the session with the physio, so that way we can work more on my left shoulder.

I am all for the speedy recovery process, I am fed up and I am tired of being physically impaired. Here's another dark and unacceptable thought I've been stewing on recently, I've already been isolating and social distancing for the last twelve months and now with this corona virus restrictions it seems to be getting harder every day that's because my wife spends a lot more time at home with me!

With my current mental situation my tolerance levels gone down even lower, I seem to find a fault in everything she does, without having any control I find myself in a foul and terrible mood, very hard to accept I wish I could help it, before the corona virus restrictions at least my wife was able to visit her family and friends and go to bingo once or twice a week and that's when I was able to get some alone time, time to think and time to process with whatever is going on in and around my life.

I guess what I'm trying to say is that I'm more angry now and I can feel the anger is creating sadness within my head and in my heart, even though I know my wife is doing her absolute best to handle me to the best of her ability I still make her feel uncomfortable around me, I don't mean it I just can't help it, I hope one day for my wife I will find an appropriate and profuse apology rightfully and meaningfully, one good thing at the moment is that I am somehow in control of my violent side from inflicting harm to anyone, although it comes close at times than I consider the circumstances and the consequences of my angry outburst and then I back off, I just got to keep backing off.

I still can't talk to anyone about any of this so therefore unfortunately the putative cause of my misery will always remain in the dark.

April 19, 2020.
Today it's the black anniversary of what could have been this time last year, so I'm a bit lost and sad, I don't want to do anything today, I don't even want to think, it hurts.

April 20, 2020.
I had a session with the psychologist this morning, I can't remember what we spoke about, just so many blanks and four pm this afternoon appointment with the hand therapist again so many blanks, the only thing I remember is going to both of them and back was with a taxi, even in the taxi it was complete silence, today is one of those days I don't know what to think, I don't know what to say and I don't know what to do, just a quite day and night in silence.

Again the tears are rolling down my face I'm in fear of crashing so somehow I need to steer my ship away from these stormy waters into the smooth sailing calm waters, maybe someday.

April 24, 2020.
Restless and unsettled the last few days, when I find my mind is drifting away with deep and dark thoughts and feel myself slipping into darkness deeper that's when it becomes extremely difficult to snap out of it calmly and smoothly, it seems to take days to recover to a very small percentage of normality, in that drifted state here are some of the thoughts I've managed to put on couple of pieces of paper.

I find myself being annoyed and really bothered, at this point of my life all I'm interested is to get my injuries fixed and get my head back in order, between all my treaters I still find myself like a leaf in the storm, for instance in the next six to eight weeks I will be having consultations with independent medical examiner, independent psychiatric examiner arranged by the insurer, forearm surgeon, work injury Doctor, my regular psychiatrist, my regular psychologist, the hand therapist, shoulder surgeon, regular physiotherapist, insurers case manager.

Miss X and my lawyers have organized for me to see independent medical examiner and independent psychiatric examiner and for me to see the lawyers, I would be naive to think that these professionals are cheap and they are humanitarians, no far from it.

They are making excellent living out of people like myself who have sad and sorry cases, I don't believe there are genuine concerns in any way shape or form from any of them it's just a bureaucratic formality, the only one that would be genuinely concerned about my wellbeing and recovery is me.

I have a strong understanding and acceptance of my physical recovery after the surgeries I've had, but the healing of the mind and the spirit is much more complex than a lot of people can't comprehend unless you find someone that's on the same path as you are. And then there are moments in my days or nights where I'm faced with some emotions of feeling ashamed and embarrassed of what I almost done twice.

I get very annoyed and soon turns into being overly angry to the point that this is the time where I want and need some positive answers for where I am and why am I here, I want some action, and in time the need for action turns into an insatiable hunger for violence, so this is why I've eliminated two of my unregistered tools, no one knows about this, I might talk about it some other time, but for now I'd like to think that I'm lucky and grateful that some part of my brain is still in control to deter me away from circumstantial desires with dire consequences.

I think the reason I hold back from some of the undesirable actions is that I'm still hopeful that one day I will find my purpose I will love life again and hopefully I will find the reasons to live again, and maybe the reasons to live will outweigh the reasons not to live, maybe I will find out that I actually belong, I don't want to be a weed anymore, I truly want to get back to my cheerful self again, I want to love and be loved again, but I'm just sitting here in a very dark and isolated place in the last twelve months ever so patiently to see the light again, so even though I do have the ideations of self harm at times and to seriously harm some people but I do think I have some control to keep the pilot light from igniting, you see a lot of these thoughts and feelings I cannot talk to anyone about them not even my psychiatrist or my psychologist.

Even though there's a Doctor and patient confidentiality I still can't trust anyone with these thoughts and feelings go through my mind, yeah I know I keep saying one day and one day and I am hoping that day will come sooner then I will ever anticipate, but for the moment I except that I have no other choice but to wait ever so patiently.

April 29, 2020.

Independent medical examination today in the city organized by the insurer, taxi there and back, not much more happening outside of my confined space, continuously stewing in my undesirable thoughts, just another day close to I don't what yet, the point of my life I am in at the moment is like being in a waiting room, what am I waiting for? And where am I going? I don't know.

I am at a point right now is that I need to keep my emotions under control, lock them up and put extra padlocks on them, so therefore I could have a day or a night without fear and without useless tears rolling down my face.

May 2, 2020.

Up and out of bed very early this morning, just another restless night, five am at the moment, I've already had four coffees and about eight cigarettes just been sitting outside and it's cold and wet, just sitting here and thinking alone where it's harmless and safe

The main thing goes through my mind at the moment is that there's no hope, there's no future and there's no resolution, I just can't help thinking and feeling this way, if I could help it I would, and yes oh yes I would dearly love to write some good things and some happy thoughts, but unfortunately I don't have bantering abilities at the moment, so maybe it's a good thing that I don't associate so I don't spread my misery onto others.

For now I am in the process of learning and understanding that there's no manifestation or fabrication for love and happiness, anyway I want to write a lot more but I'm tired, mentally knocked about and knocked around so much so that my head feels like it's completely bruised.

May 4, 2020.
Another psychologist session this morning with nothing gained and nothing lost, with my current head space being so muddled up that concentrating levels are right down so anything I want to do mentally becomes fruitless, no fault of the psychologist when the concentrating, learning and understanding mechanisms are switched off that was the case with me this morning.

Then the hand therapist this afternoon, except he performed professional task appropriately on my left forearm and that was it mostly silent, I don't have the willingness or the ability to associate even with the medical professionals at the moment, I wish I could stop being so despondent.

Anyway, I've attended both of my appointments today with taxies that was generously supplied by the insurer, so the rest of the day and night starting to feel like a full time job where I do two eight hour shifts in the office with my miserable thoughts and trying to write something sensible on my daily report but no avail again.

May 6 2020.
Today I don't want to write about my night last night and how got out of bed this morning, it brings me down and keeps me down so that it almost becomes just another justification point to my miserable state, anyway something different.

I had a phone consultation with the WI Dr this morning where there was no value in it at all, and an hour later had another phone consultation with the forearm surgeon, again with no value at all, both of the phone consultations felt a bit like a social call where they both wanted to know how I'm travelling, well I guess I could have told them both anything.

Whether they believe me or not may not have any importance, now the main question would be did these two phone consultations took place by dictatorially instigated for financial advantages?

One would never know I guess, once again I apologize for thinking like this and being so critical but I believe strongly that in the corporate world you don't receive anything for nothing, besides I do have a lot of time in my recovery process and spend a lot of time on my own that my mind can wander off to so many different directions.

May 8, 2020.
Physio this morning, we take the splint off of the left forearm do some exercises and on the left shoulder as well and then the splint back on the left forearm and then back home, so that's my outing for today, long and quite day and night, hey I'm used to it, that's life for now.

May 11, 2020.
Got out of bed this morning early as usual with some strange thoughts and feelings, physically flat and nathalgic, mentally wow it's quite explosive, so many things are going through my mind at the same time with uncontrollable speed, I'll try and explain one of the topics as it goes through my mind if I can catch it and put a finger on it, well here it goes.

It feels as if my journey is coming to an end, I feel as I have nothing left to do on this earth, no point in asking myself any questions where I have no answers, with all the disappointments, let downs, back stabbings, hurt and physical pain that's creating a deep dark anger, the anger that's hungry and thirsty for some accountability and for resolution that can be used as a life line that can help me dig myself out of my miserable darkness, as I constantly think about all this day in day out that it really points me and almost drags me into the direction of severe and savage revenge.

Well, I've never asked or volunteered to be in this deep, dark and lonely place that I've been in the last fourteen months, however I am thankful that I can keep this powerful urge under control with great difficulty, so I am trying to write and reveal more and more of what's inside the walls of my mind with the encouragement of my psychologist that it may help me to cope with it all, yeah for this I will give her credit that some days I do find a bit of comfort in writing and yes it does keep me calm, however I am still cautiously reluctant to reveal some serious issues yet, maybe in the near future but for now I'm scared that if my notebook falls into wrong hands I really don't want anything on these pages to be held against me if an undesirable event arises.

Anyway, it has not been an easy ride since it all began March last year, it's been a long, lonely, sad lots of downs not enough ups and very hurtful ride in many aspects.

I am finding out another thing while all this is happening is the way I seem to be handling myself and I am realizing that I have this power this strength that's deterring me away from regrettable actions and making useless mistakes that I might never be able to forgive myself, yeah I'm glad to be thinking and writing about all this today, I feel there's a certain degree of optimism is kicking in to keep me being hopeful that it's all going to get better and that I will find my purpose again I will smile and be happy again, I will grab the reigns and continue on my peaceful journey again, oh one very important issue for me is my wife, she is not educated or trained and she's not a paid professional when it comes to mental health issues, so for her to understand my situation or what I'm going through.

I know for a fact it's extremely hard for her to deal with me I know at times I can be totally unreasonable with her that I can't control, it doesn't matter how profusely I can apologize or how remorseful I am it still hurts and upsets me, I give her hundred percent credit I'm sure that she doesn't want her loving husband in this shape at all, again I'm optimistic that one day I will have the opportunity to make it all up to her, well these are my thoughts for today, what I think of and what I write have became the main activities of my days and nights that seems to keep me calm for some reason.

May 16, 2020.
Two days ago I misunderstood the appointment details with the forearm surgeon, instead of me going into seeing him we ended up having the consultation by phone, just a check up so it was okay

and he wants to see me again start of next month, and yesterday I've seen the psychiatrist it was a very short consultation as usual and the only important thing was he wanted a copy of the independent medical examiners report from last month.

There was nothing else important enough for me to remember, and today seen the physio early this morning, we worked mainly on the left shoulder and done some extensive movements that felt good and positive, it felt like we're starting to make good progress with the left shoulder not much with the forearm yet, more patients.

Anyhow, still getting up early in the mornings with very little sleep, getting up with high levels of emotions, the emotions there are running wild in my head inevitably turns into high level of anger where it disturbs my concentration on keeping the lid on for some undesirable actions, so obviously this brings my moods right down to the point that I have no expectations on anything good or positive eventuating.

I feel that I have to learn to live with my current situation or find a way to use every strand of my inner and outer strength to change the course of my own direction and be in charge in control of my destiny, yeah one day, so I am desperate so desperate for answers and solutions to get me out of this deep and dark hole that at times I feel I'm running out of time and patience.

I just don't know what to do or how to do anything about it, I am starting to look into the sky's with my level of worshipping asking and begging the powers above for mercy and for resolution, it feels as if I have nowhere else left to turn to, so from here on I don't know how long but I have a strong suspicion that it will be a lot of blanks for a while.

Chapter 21

May 18, 2020.
Big day today with two appointments, first the psychologist and then the hand therapist, well firstly a very heavy session with the psychologist, half way through the session I mention to her that I had two firearms.

Firstly she informed me that confidentiality rule can be broken by her if it need to be and then she asked me if they were registered and then she asked me why did I feel the need to tell her about them and do I still have them, wow and wow I thought why did I mention them to her.

I took a couple of deep breaths and paused for few minutes, and then when I regained my composure I started telling her that I don't have them anymore and the reason of me telling her about them is that I trusted her, I haven't told anyone about them and I'm not about to, because I don't associate with anyone at the moment I must have felt the need to talk to someone about them, not that I needed any clarification as to why or why not have them but I don't know why I've mentioned them to her.

Anyway, the session ended on a good note even though she was concerned but she still gave me a constructive advice to keep it together and keep calm, oh by the way I did not mention to her that the twelfth of October last year I was in a full rage and went to do something catastrophic that I had them with me and that I wasn't going to come home that day, actually I haven't told anyone about this yet.

Maybe I should be scared to talk or write about this but I'm only trying to be open and honest about all my thoughts and feelings,

I'm not trying to sound like a hero and I certainly am not a survivor because this is not a game but at the same time I don't want to incriminate myself, so these are some serious reasons why I spend a lot of time on my own that I can't speak to anyone, and every time I mention something or reveal something that's heavy and emotional on these pages it really takes me back to those moments and I get to relive the painful moments second by second that really gets me down even deeper that can take a few days to catch my breath.

Maybe it's a good thing that I spend a lot of time on my own, even if I wanted to I wouldn't be able to communicate with anyone for now.

May 22, 2020.
Physio this morning, well that was the only activity in my day today, last few days very quiet, blank in so many areas in my head and feeling down and I don't know what's it going to be like the next few days.

I don't have the mental capacity at the moment to pay any attention to anything, just the usual stuff, coffees, cigarettes, pain killers and antidepressants, all these negativities, painful days and nights, not seeing a light at the end of the tunnel and nothing on the horizon truly makes the fine line between staying or leaving very intense, this has been too long that I've been feeling like this.

I can't and I don't want to live like this anymore so I need to choose which way I want to go and make a firm decision soon, yeah it's up to me, I guess I have the power to choose whichever way I want to go, I hope I make the right choice whichever one it is, either erase it all and wipe it clean or continue my journey until the end with some satisfying normality with my family.

May 26 2020. I am deeply saddened by the news I've received this morning that my brother-in-law had passed away two days ago, may god rest him in peace, really good man and I have a lot of respect for him, not in the mood for anything else.

June 3, 2020.
Seen the psychologist yesterday, the session was mild and pleasant, I don't know what I've done or how but I feel the respect levels are escalating, maybe it's a good thing that I can use all the respect I can get to my advantage as a first step to my recovery process to pull me out of my darkness.

Anyhow, seen the work injury doctor this morning, I've received a good reception from her as well, even though we're in pandemic the consultation was face to face, she gave me non capacity forms for another two weeks and told me that we will have a discussion about return to work program on the seventeenth of this month.

I was happy with her attitude she wasn't judgemental and she wasn't intimidating, and then early this afternoon I've seen the forearm surgeon, it was the same reception with him and good vibes all good, maybe with attitudes like this from all my medical treaters will respectfully elevate my optimism and give me some hope, one can only hope, same with him it was face to face consultation and taxi there and back as well with the generosity of the insurer.

June 4 2020.
Seen the hand therapist this afternoon, a gentle and mild moves and exercises with my left arm and while this is happening I mentioned to him that Miss X was organizing a return to work program for me.

He told me that he needs to be part of the program and that if I can inform Miss X and that was it for today, oh taxi there and back, I'm starting to lose count on how many taxies I've been in since the start of all this, that's life, it's not a game and it's not a joke.

June 5, 2020.
Two appointments this morning, physio and psychologist, unfortunately with me not being in the mood I cannot comment on the worthiness of this morning's appointments, just blank, oh taxies there and back again.

June 11, 2020.
Two appointments again this morning, physio and psychologist, same as the last time, again no comment, it is sad that I have lost my conceptual skills for the moment that I'm finding it hard to engage in productive conversations.

It is and has been one of my problems for the last fifteen months, but I am trying to deal with it as well as other concerning issues in my head, I wish I could sweep it all under the carpet, but hey there's no carpet so I'll keep on sweeping my issues around and around in my head until they all disappear one day, wishful thinking, anyway taxies to my appointments and back, how lucky am I?

June 12, 2020.
I've seen an independent medical examiner this morning that was arranged by my lawyers, I think that my lawyers are under the impression that this is all coming to an end so that there's a claim can be made for pain and suffering where there could be some financial gain for both myself and offcourse the lawyers.

My main concern is that I want acknowledgement and accountability for being bullied and harassed in my work place, I guess I need to trust my lawyers, we'll see what happens.

June 13, 2020.
Still having very little and limited sleep, even though the pain on both the left shoulder and the forearm is at a good manageable level with pain killers I still can't sleep on my left side.

It gets me annoyed, broken sleep obviously triggers my mind and puts it in overload, thinking of a lot of things like my social life it is almost at its lowest levels, I am starting to feel like a social reject but at the same time it is so tiering trying to stay focused on anything, every single person is getting on my nerves, that includes my wife, I get fearful at times I don't know if she's had enough of my moods and my uselessness and she's going to walk away or is it me going to walk away for good.

There's so much going through my head but I just can't talk to anyone, well for a start no one seems to have the time and the ones that do have the time show no concern or interest in what I may be talking about, so I do end up believing that the world is a very lonely place, the life itself is lonely, right now I don't believe I'll ever get back to normal.

It feels as if this is a new way of living I don't like it and I don't seem to be handling it well at all but I'm still searching, I don't want to give up but I don't know how long can I keep going like this, mentally I feel very tired I've had enough, I know I shouldn't think and feel like this but I just can't help it, it starting to feel that it is becoming more and more powerful that I'm starting to except it is becoming beyond my control, the worrying question is How Long?

June 17, 2020.
Physio yesterday, just as usual, even though I feel it's a very slow process in my physical recovery I keep getting told by the physio that we're making good progress, well I guess there's a bit of a positivity there that can lift my spirits up, I need a lot more of this

I've seen the WI Dr this morning, again it was just a formality what they call it a routine check up, well for me it is just one of those instructions where I must attend other ways I am being threatened by the consequences of my weekly payment being reduced or declined altogether so I have to attend every appointment wether I like it or not wether I can or not, it's a must.

Anyway, taxies there and back again.

June 18, 2020.
Hand therapist today, he asked me to increase the exercise for my left forearm from five times a day to ten times a day and keep on wearing the splint continuously on my arm for a while and that his treatment can take up to six months, he does not want to rush the treatment so we don't go backwards.

I'll be seeing him again on the second of July. Taxies there and back

June 19, 2020.
Up again very early this morning, loosing track of time where I don't look at the clock when I get out of bed, after a long and heavy battles I've been having in my thoughts department where I've been body slammed, kicked, walked on, disrespected, discarded repeatedly again and again, but today I've decided that I will put some constructiveness in my day and in my thoughts but before I do here are some of the thoughts I've dealt with all day since way before the sun came up.

Firstly I truly need to reduce and in some cases stop the pills I'm taking, one of them is the antidepressants, I have made the decision as of today I will not take them anymore knowing for a fact that they don't work for me, I strongly believe that it's a formula to numb my scull in a twenty four cycle and towards the end of the cycle where the effect is wearing off I take another antidepressant pill to keep my scull numb for another twenty four hours, and this goes on for how long I wouldn't know or whenever I get told to stop taking them

I also know for a fact since I've started taking them I've became like a zombie where I don't have much control in my thoughts and feelings, and tonight I will stop taking sleeping pills, well I get out of bed early and different hours every morning, if I can't stay in bed and sleep what's the point in taking sleeping pills every night, wether these two are clashing with the pain killers I'm taking at the same time I don't know but the ones that are prescribing them to me know about the mixture of pills I'm on but they don't say anything to me, if anything I get encouraged to keep on taking them.

I guess it would be in my best interest to monitor myself in the next few days. Here are some of the reasons why I've come to such strong conclusions is that since I've injured myself early twenty thirteen I've been on pain killers on and off for a while but early April last year when I started to take antidepressants together with the pain killers is when it all started and I did have strong suicidal ideations in the first three weeks and almost went through with it, ever since and often and some weeks almost every day I live with so many mixed emotions like I have became a despondent person I don't have a clear vision my way of thinking is always disturbed with lots of negatives nothing positive, nothing has any worthiness, no love, no concern and I still find myself slipping in to dangerous thoughts about suicidal ideations and questioning myself like is it ones right? Is it a privilege? When, where, why and how does one contemplate the ideation?

We will never know, does one have the power the strength the courage to go through with it? and does one also have the power the strength and the courage not to go through with it? so if we do get answers to any of these questions, are they speculative and assumingly gathered knowledge? We will never know.

One thing I've learned and excepted respectfully is that the people who contemplate suicidal ideations are not silly they are not stupid and they are not idiots, They are desperate people with nowhere to go and no one to turn to, the reason I know this is because I've been called silly and I've been told that what I've contemplated was idiotic, anyway I truly don't know why I constantly think about all this, when and where will all this end.

At the moment late at night while I'm drinking my coffee I'm wandering do I look forward to tomorrow, next week, next month or next year? No I don't, do I make plans? No I don't, but for me to look to the future and make plans I need to communicate with people, I need to rely on people, I need to start trusting people, I need to learn to live again, I need to learn to love again and I need to get interested in life itself again.

But the mind set I have at the moment none of the above can be possible, it's not that I forcefully block myself from good possibilities in life it just happens, it really is a constant struggle, especially in the last six months the painful and the miserable events I've experienced, some of them are I've caused some expensive damage in the back yard, I almost threw a chair through a window, I've dropped coffee mugs and plates of food on the floors thinking that I have confidence in my left arm thinking that I won't feel any pain I was wrong, walking into doors and door jams with my bandaged arm and bandaged shoulder at other times, and once or twice I've build up enough confidence to drive to my mum's only to find out what it had felt like I woke up and found myself doing one hundred kilometres an hour on the freeway not knowing where I'm going and why, oh boy that was frightening.

So I still entertain the thought the idea of ending it all at once but this time I don't want to do it alone, I desperately want to take some people with me, but at the same time I am hoping that it's only an idea it's only a thought that I don't ever want to find myself in a position to action any ideation at all.

Now talking about constructiveness in my day, I need to start using my self control strength, I need to start mastering the calmness and enter into my thoughts one at a time, I need to stop peoples insignificant actions putting me into more sombre mood, and more importantly I would like to start believing and excepting that I am strong and powerful enough to take control of my emotions, what has happened in the last fourteen months is inconceivable, so if I don't get myself out of this imperceptible motion that there's a very good chance of me being stuck on the treadmill of self destruction for many years to come.

So once again life goes on and I don't want to be a leaf in the storm anymore. Thinking and writing about all this today and tonight I've just realized that I've entered into the early hours of the morning with tears in my eyes, I just hope that the tears are from overwhelming joy that there's a possibility of me guiding myself into the direction of where I may want to be, I need to go and get some rest now and hopefully tomorrow I will still have the same optimism to pick me up, build me up and bring me to where I was once.

June 22, 2020.

Seen the psychologist this morning, it was a good session and we recapitulated on some important issues, it was intense at times and yet it became exhilarating too, and some of what we've discussed was of the record but ended well.

Anyway, as I'm starting to find some courage and strength to feed, Pump and exercise my optimism to change my direction as I'm coming home driving my wife's car a guy coming out of a driveway hits my wife's car on the left rear near the boot section, well I thought I didn't need this today and when we started to exchange names and phone numbers he was remorseful and admitted fault so there was no need for my anger levels to rise.

It was a good thing for me to stay optimistically on my path, early days and baby steps, I just want to see where it takes me, I need to really stay focused on my patience and my calmness if there's ever a chance for me to get out of where I am at the moment.

June 23, 2020.

Seen the physio early this morning, not much to get excited about, slow process with a little positivity.

I am at the point of acceptance that my left shoulder and my left forearm will never be one hundred percent back to what it was before the injuries but I will wait and see patiently. And seen the psychiatrist this afternoon the conversation was short and useless and the next appointment will be twenty sixth of August.

This again confirms to me that he is helping himself financially through my situation, he is not helping me at all, but that's another issue I cannot allow it to put any obstacles on my path for the moment but in saying this I found out this afternoon that I've lost over four hundred dollars from my weekly payment as of today, well that didn't go down too well at all, well as much as I want to get out my darkness with some positive energy, but losing that amount out of my pay was a huge negative, after all I am trying to improve my mental state and I'm doing all I can for a full physical recovery so is this what it feels like getting a financial kick in the guts when you're already down and just about out.

I can yell I can scream I can swear til the cows come home but that won't achieve anything, just got to keep calm and accept the fact that in our system there are standard operating procedures that have been ruthlessly put together and presented to people on the ground floor like myself, now these rule makers are not interested in the fact that I did not contribute to my injuries and I didn't ask to be bullied and harassed at my work place to the point where I cannot control my emotions, losing that amount out of my weekly pay is not acceptable but there's nothing I can do about it.

The best I can do at the moment is to stay focused and try to keep myself under control, I just hope the rest of the afternoon and night I have the power not to let it get out of control, I will do my best

June 24, 2020.

Got up early this morning after a usual night of turning and tossing and not getting enough sleep I took my cigarettes and my cup of coffee and went outside in the backyard where I do a lot of my thinking in a peaceful environment and one of the first thing for me is to pay attention this morning was to monitor my moods now that I've stopped taking the antidepressants and the sleeping pills a few days ago.

Maybe it's still early days but I don't feel any different, I'm hoping that it will get better from here on and I will keep on monitoring myself. I do realize and gracefully except that I only I alone can get myself out of this darkness.

It is imperative that I ignore peoples useless assumptions and opinions and their speculative inputs where it's already extremely hard trying to do it on my own without any useless hurdles on my path. Anyway finding out about my wage reduction yesterday not knowing what to do or who to turn to I thought I'll start with calling the unions that I am a member of, and to my surprise I was told that discussions about weekly pay was not their area of expertise

Okay, lets go to plan B I thought, I've called the insurer and spoke to my case manager about it, and the way he explained it to me that he talked a lot but said nothing, well that was fruitless, lastly I thought I'll call my lawyers, and guess what yeah that was pointless and waste of time.

So yes there's a lot of negativity here, being on one wage in my household and the reduction of large portion of my wage certainly does put a lot of pressure on my head about all the living expenses, well this could be another negative hurdle on my path but if I'm serious about getting myself off of this path full of negativities I need to do all I can to achieve this, even if it means that I will use every bit of my strength to get me back on the surface again.

I think a lot about all this and I write about all this and I am at the point now that I don't want to think about any of this anymore, I want to turn a new page in my life, ohhhh, I am tired I will stop here with tears in my eyes again.

June 25, 2020.

Seen the physio early this morning, we worked on my left shoulder, some pain at times but it was okay, didn't do much on my left forearm, I still have my forearm in a splint all good.

From physio I went to work on light duties for three hours for the first time this year. Well the reception was very cold and I think it might have been inevitable to me that the people I've worked with so many years was somewhat avoiding me, it was almost a big effort to get a smile or a simple hello, but with me being determent to stay on my path to my mental recovery that I felt I needed to stay calm and use as much energy and strength as it takes to stay positive, over all I know and except that I don't have many options.

Anyhow, as much as I want to stay calm and positive I've noticed that in the duration of three hours I was at work today not one load on any of the trucks were getting checked in the loading bays, now March last year the truck that I've loaded was allegedly not checked and according to my managers statement that I've lied about the truck that I've loaded was checked by me was the main reason why I've received a first and final written warning and further to my shock one of my team members who has mental health issues and only attends to work six months of the year has become second in charge running the loading bays.

I thought mmmmm, this is going to take extra strength and patience and this is the guy that swore at me twice before my surgeries and at the time of me having suicidal ideations, well this is not received and excepted too well by me but I've kept quiet so there's no unnecessary problems or troubles, although it's hard to keep calm keep my cool and falsely smile at people I am serious about getting myself out of my misery so yes I am using a lot of my inner strength and it is taking a lot of powerful effort to get to the light at the end of my tunnel, even if it's the longest tunnel I have to crawl on my hands and knees to see the light I want to do it.

I want to add a lot of optimism into my determination now! On the brighter note though I should be happy with my attitude that somehow I am finding the ability to handle the ostracizing that I'm receiving at my work place much calmly, at the moment I need more of these kind of positivity's in my life if I want to get myself out of my miserable state, for the moment I think these are the tools that comes from within that might be able to help me.

Nothing else and no one else will have the ability or the power to understand or help me in any way, simply because I left myself open to opprobrium and lost my balance and fell in too deep, so it is entirely up to me to find my way out of this.

June 26, 2020.

Out of bed early again this morning, no changes in my sleeping patterns and no difference in my moods, even though I've stopped taking sleeping pills and antidepressants about a week ago I don't feel any different.

After yesterdays ordeal at my work place the ostracizing and the dramatic changes in the loading bays where none of the trucks being checked led me to believe that I was deliberately targeted in March twenty nineteen where I received first and final written warning, oh boy this inevitably allowed my mind to wander off in so many different directions all afternoon and night yesterday until the early hours of this morning, I just did not have the ability to stop the mixed emotions of feeling weak, useless, inadequate and mostly teary, it really is not easy where I feel hurt I feel lost I feel betrayed I feel let down I feel very angry where there's a powerful feeling of being in a dead end situation where there's no way out.

It's that feeling again where my mind goes completely silent, all of the thoughts have disappeared, I feel scared very scared of the pilot light reigniting, I feel scared of losing control, as much as I honour my responsibilities and the circumstances that I'm in and the consequences of what I might action it really isn't easy to keep it together, but hey I'm not going to except that my problems have no solutions, I don't want to give up, I want to work at it no matter how long it takes.

Hey, I realized I was lucky enough to receive my life and I really don't want to give it back before it's due date. Anyway there's the weekend approaching where I can concentrate on keeping calm and staying on top of my anger issues.

June 29, 2020.

I had a face time consultation with an independent psychiatric examiner today that was arranged by my lawyer.

I thought the examining was rushed he looked and sounded like he was preoccupied with other things on his mind, while I was mentioning few things during consultation he kept cutting in to my sentence and telling me that we will come back to it but never did, so I'm not comfortable with the report he'll be presenting to my lawyer, we'll see what happens.

I guess like everyone else he has to justify his earnings too, anyway not long after I got off the phone with the psychiatrist I had a bit of a moment, I became emotional and teary that I had to be examined by a psychiatrist, never ever in all my years have I thought that I would be examined by a psychiatrist, I guess I'm finding it hard to except and hard to forgive the people that put me in this situation, but hey life goes on and it must.

July 1 2020.

Physio this morning, just a usual routine of exercise and a mild massage on the left shoulder, and the rest of the day and night just trying to keep calm without any negative thoughts, and trying not to turn excuses into reasons for me to get upset unnecessarily, these are the tools I've created and that I'm working them.

I am serious about getting myself out of my darkness, let's face it if I don't help myself and if I can't create helpful and useful tools for my situation that I know of very well than no one else will, I've come to understand and except that words and pills don't work for me, only tools will, I mean we don't build bridges and buildings with words, we do use appropriate tools where ever necessary, however trying to find the right tools haven't been easy, it's not easy and I don't believe it will be an easy task but I have to start somewhere.

I have to find at least the first tool in the hopeful optimism that more and more tools will flow through into my area so that I can choose them and use them carefully to help me through, I don't want to give in, I don't want to give up and I don't want to let go now but hey this is what I feel and how I feel right now, I don't know what tomorrow will bring so therefore I don't want to make any promises that I can't keep, again this is where it gets hard not having confidence in what tomorrow will bring has a way of keeping me on the tread mill of self destruction much longer than I could have anticipated.

Every now and then getting a little glimpse or a little spur of optimism about anything is like a candle light on a windy night where it doesn't stay on long enough for me to see anything or hold on to anything, anyway we'll see what happens tomorrow.

July 2 2020.
Seen the work injury doctor this morning, it was a good consultation.

I felt that she showed me due respect and understanding and explained to me that I don't have to go to work tomorrow, but Miss X was up to her old tricks again trying to overturn the Doctors recommendations and with a little bit of aggression pushing me to go to work tomorrow, after a little conversation with Miss X on the phone she almost got me to the point of hyper verbal vocabulary that I had to hang up the phone, next time I see or speak with Miss X I will strongly suggest to her to stay off and away from my radar

I have no intentions of violence against her but I can't help feeling scared that should she ever push me to the limit where I might not be responsible for my actions, I know for a fact consequences would be dreadful for Miss X, I would strongly recommend that people like Miss X should regularly undergo an intense refresher course especially on improving their " people skills " so they don't put themselves or others at risk of injury, you see the attitude of people like Miss X can be quite hazardous to my mental state, just a short conversation on the phone today with Miss X has ignited some dangerous and violent thoughts in my head, not good at all at a time when I'm trying to pick myself up and start to move forward

I truly don't need any hurdles on my path right now. Anyway seen the hand therapist this afternoon we are making slow but good progress with my left forearm, taxi's again today to both of my appointments supplied by the insurer.

The rest of the day and night I concentrated strongly on the idea of resisting to pay useless attention on Miss X's unwarranted and unprofessional attitude so that I can stay calm and hoping that I'll have a better day tomorrow to work on my mental recovery.

July 3, 2020.

I was meant have a phone conversation/ appointment at nine am this morning with an official from the insurer, however I didn't received the call until ten forty am.

No apologies no worries that's okay, so I told this lady from the insurers customer care department about Miss X being so unprofessional no people skills and no compassion, it's all about pushing me to go back to work no matter what no consideration for my situation or my wellbeing and similar with my current case manager of the insurer that at times I feel that I've been patronized and at some point even a bit of sarcasm and in the past fifteen months I've had ten different case managers, and at the end of the meeting she assured me that she will look in to it and get to the bottom of all this, well I'm not holding my breath we'll see what happens and how long.

Hopefully one day this is all going to end and I hope it ends well, I truly don't want to do anything out of the ordinary, I don't want to hurt anyone, I don't want to go to jail and I don't want to be six foot under, I just want to be able to see the rest of my journey on this earth in peace, I do want to have a genuine smile on my face again and I do want to love and socialize again.

I guess one can always hope for the best no matter what the outcome is at times.

July 6, 2020.
Even though the physical pain is at a good manageable point with less pain killers I still go through my days and nights with mixed emotions, too many to mention at the moment but one of them is my agoraphobic state that I can't seem to get myself out of my confined space to socialize with anyone.

I am using a lot of my strength to keep myself mild and calm, maybe being in my confined space is the reason why I am managing to keep mildly calm I just don't know and I can't bring myself to be open to any speculative assumptions for the moment.

Knowing my own miserable issues of anger, resentment, regrets, feeling worthless, feeling useless and ideations of self harm and harm others, it's not easy to live with these emotions, this is big this is powerful and this is very real, well in saying all that I feel that I am coming to a very powerful point in my life where I need to make the decision the decision to stay on my journey or to remove myself from all of my miseries for good, now I can think of some reasons why I should give up and let go, but are they valid enough are they powerful enough or strong enough to push me over the edge?

For this very moment I don't know, but maybe, just maybe I should pay more attention to the things and people in my life that are much much more valuable and much more important to me than I've ever given them credit for, maybe in the immediate future if I did pay more attention to the values in my life and if I allow myself to except that these values are strong enough and valid enough and really believe that, than I may be able to walk away from the edge that at times terrifies me.

For me to make the decision the achievable decision to walk away from the edge I guess I need to work on getting myself out of my agoraphobic state, I need to lose the fear, the fear of winning or losing, I need to start understanding that this is not a game this is not a competition, this is a battle I need to fight face to face head on if I want to resurface again and breathe again, so yeah there's a battle ahead and it's entirely up to me to make the suitable decision, I am in the clear understanding that talking is cheap and assumptions are useless, as I said all along I have the inner strength I have the power, but today I actually realized that I still have the power I've just lost the ability to use it.

I have a long night ahead for me to work on the idea of using my powers appropriately on where, when and how, I will not wish myself any luck to get me out of this because luck had nothing to do with me being pushed in to the deep end, it is the narcissistic people who are responsible for me been in this situation for the last sixteen months, however I need to deal with this issue calmly and appropriately when the time is right, I understand that I have serious issues and I also understand that if I want to resolve any of them I need to prioritize them to achieve reasonably satisfactory resolutions.

July 8 2020.

Physio early this morning not much different just a normal routine exercises, I'm just doing what needs to be done to get more strength on my left shoulder and my left forearm.

I've seen my family Doctor this afternoon for an annual check up, and the rest of the day and night I'm starting to work on my defence mechanism like ducking, weaving and jumping over hurdles like an elite athlete, knowing but hoping not to be put into the predicament where I can't handle the situation and myself as calmly as possible.

I wish I could be confident about all this but I'm trying and for this I can take a little bit of credit for what It's worth, apart from all this It is a quite day and night, still no socialising and I still spend most of my time in my confined space, I think it's safe and I believe it's helping me with my calmness and that's what matters at the moment without sugar coating anything.

July 9 2020.

I went to work this morning for three hours on light duties but my manager was under the impression that I'll be in tomorrow not today so he found some work for me in the office doing some photo copying and scanning, however I've experienced something very disturbing and downgrading today, well a few years ago I started this thing about buying a lottery ticket whenever it jackpotted, with me collecting five dollars from my team members and a couple of the staff from the office.

I would purchase the lottery ticket make copies and distribute to all that's involved and if one of my team member was not attending work that day I would take a photo of the ticket and text it to them, so the duration of me been absent I was not included and when I asked the question to one of my team members which also happens to be a good friend of mine actually lied to my face telling me that he's been putting money in for me and about ten minutes later I found out from another team member that it wasn't true.

Wow, that was disappointing and hurtful, well as I am trying to dig myself out of the dark hole I ought to control my emotions and not inject any useless energy into this issue to become bigger issue than what it's worth, yes there will come a time where I might forgive but I will not allow myself to forget so that I can carefully select who I can be friends with and who I can trust.

I will not pay any more attention to this as it can play on my mind and drag me down with it. Well maybe there's an element of amusement in my head that I'm not on the bottom of my darkness but in saying that I'm not out of the woods yet, I know it may take a long time before I get myself right out of my darkness completely but I will endeavour to use as much power, patients and strength as it needs.

July 13, 2020.
Seen the psychologist this morning, the main topic today was about relaxing and meditation to keep calm, once again I've explained to the psychologist that I need more time and I need to be ready to be able to connect and concentrate on any of the meditation program for me to achieve satisfactory results, it was understood and accepted by the psychologist so she gave me the names of some programs there are available on line for me to have a look when I'm ready.

Anyway, just as I am trying to keep neutral in my mental state not to get too excited and not to pay too much attention on any of the negative stuff a delivery van hit the car that I'm driving on the left rear.

When I got out of the car and exchanged names and phone numbers and then got back in the car and took off, wow I thought, I was proud of myself for not losing my cool and kept calm the whole time.

Maybe I need to keep this attitude going if I need to resurrect what's almost destroyed, well the rest of the day and night I should be able to pay more attention on staying neutral and staying calm for as long as it takes.

Chapter 22

July 16, 2020.
Physio yesterday new exercises it feels like slow process but we're getting there I need to be more patient, back to work today for another three hours on light duties, it was a very cold reception it feels as if everyone was working alone, people were like robots no respect no bond very flat indeed.

For me I find it absolutely useless being there, I know they are trying to get me back to work but at least I should be over ninety percent recovered and ready, oh well I'll just go along with it, I will not allow it to play on my mind if I want to protect my mental state

I am doing my best to regain the ability to use my powers again to overcome not one but all of my issues, and I have seen the hand therapist this afternoon, well without being negative he is doing a great work on my left forearm but telling me that he needs to treat my forearm for another six months, really?

I thought am I a good candidate to be milked a little longer or am I being unfair and negatively reading too much in to it, I need to stop being negative as I know it can and will inject unnecessary energy into my already troubled head, again taxi there and back and I actually lost count on how many taxi's I've travelled in since this ordeal begun.

Anyway, just as I thought that was all for today I received a call from the lawyers office telling me that the lawyer who was preparing me to go to court about bullying, harassment and common law claim is no longer with the firm and they've appointed a new lawyer to look after my case, and she got on the phone telling me that my employers lawyers made an offer of some dollars, it definitely is not a life changing amount but that's beside the point, then she really put fear in me by telling me that I should except the offer and walk away not to worry about me being harassed and bullied and further more my employers lawyers will challenge that I might have contributed to my injuries and that if we do take this case to court there's a good chance we will lose and that it will cost me a lot of money, well really?

I thought my lawyers were working for me and fighting for my rights, especially for my mental state I needed some accountability some closure not to mention my physical pain and suffering

Anyway, the thought of my lawyer and my employers lawyers having some kind of hidden agenda had become highlighted in my head but unfortunately I can't prove anything so therefore I felt I had no choice and the way my lawyer spoke to me that I was obligated to except the offer so that my lawyers can get paid, and when I excepted the offer there was a condition attached to it that I had to sign a form that once I received the offer and my lawyers get twenty five percent of it then we will never open this case again or talk about it again it will be dead and buried.

As much as I was reluctant to except the offer and didn't care about the money, all I wanted was recognition and a sincere apology, it didn't happen, even though I don't want to let it but it will play some sad role in my head for a long time, thinking and feeling that whatever was done since the beginning of this ordeal by my employer and some of my colleagues is excusable and allowable, so here's another hurdle on my path to recovery that someday I may be fortunate enough to get over it, at this point I guess it would be easy for me to say that one should not hold one's breath for too long.

The sad point about all this is that there's always some external bullshit issue that comes into my head rekindles and starts the fire again where I thought I was building enough courage and strength to defuse and put out the fire, so there you go as I said all I wanted out of all this was a sincere apology and accountability, now if these were the two key elements to get me out of my dark and sad situation, well they were ignored, discarded, disregarded and disrespected, now this could have been my last crying out for help, we will never know, one thing for sure life goes on and it must.

July 20, 2020.
Seen the work injury doctor this morning, she was understanding, concerned and showed me some respect, all good it was decided that I'll work this Thursday and as of next week we'll increase it to two days a week and hopefully by the end of August we can increase it to fulltime capacity.

There's a bit of an optimism and a glimpse of hope that one day soon I will recover and I will put all this behind me, it's been a while that I haven't mentioned anything about my sleeping patterns or my pains and aches, since I've stopped taking sleeping pills and antidepressants I seem to be managing okay the only thing is that I still continue with my excessive amounts of coffee and cigarettes, still do a lot of thinking, still trying to extract some sense and some useful answers out of all this.

I still find myself in lots of dead ends, anyway on the brighter note I am very dearly thankful to the two close friends of mine that lives' thirty-six kilometres from my house and I've known them both well over forty years, they are the only ones that check up on me three to four times a week to see if I'm okay and if I need anything, they both know my story because they listen, I am thankful to have them in my life.

July 23, 2020.
Seen the physio yesterday morning and then went and seen the hand surgeon all good nothing different and today went to work for three hours on light duties, there's really nothing to talk about except it's all same old same old.

The rest of the day and night while I'm on the path of physical recovery I just can't help drifting into some of my unpleasant thoughts where it almost leaves me powerless to control my emotions with a burning rage and anger, at the moment it's three forty five in the morning here's something that I've been paying a lot of attention to, over the years I have learned that there are so many different types of mental health issues or illnesses, most common ones are anxiety disorder, schizophrenia, obsessive disorder, autism, post traumatic stress disorder, depression and the list goes on and on almost three hundred of different mental illnesses, alcoholism and gambling can be considered as a mental health issue.

The certain recommendations for a lot of these issues are antidepressants, meditation, relaxation, exercise and healthy food, and whispering sweet nothings into our ears like hey everything is going to be alright, and these are the only so called tools we have today to work with, until certain and solid tools are invented and made available we will see a lot of people with mental health issues being deteriorated, and furthermore if the right tools invented and available maybe then we would have a very good chance of preventing so many life's being lost ever so tragically and prevent families from going through the unnecessary grieving process.

In the meqan time we just sit back and watch our medical professionals and experts enlarge their wealth quite handsomely with no resolution to most of us sufferers.

Maybe this is a big and powerful statement I'm making, maybe this is all coming from the dark side that I've been for a while, maybe I'm still angry that I'm not out of the woods yet and knowing that it will be with me and in my head for a very long time, yeah at times I know I can be harshly and unfairly critical towards our medical professionals but whenever and whatever I put down on these pages are raw and pure that comes from my emotions and from my darkest times, maybe I should apologize if I hurt, upset or offend anyone but then again I don't know if it would be appropriate for me to apologize when I can't control my emotions

My anger and my thoughts, I write exactly how I feel and what I feel for that moment so I am not out to deliberately hurt, upset or offend anyone and if I do I apologize.

July 29, 2020.
Had a face time session with the psychologist this afternoon, I must not have been in the right state so the session felt useless, I just couldn't connect, I think I'm starting to become anxiously

desperate to get out of the state I'm in, I'm truly sick and tired of all this bullshit, I really don't appreciate where I am at the moment.

I find it hard to breath at times, as I said once or twice before that there's no respect no compassion no understanding, I feel this goes right across with everyone I know including with some of my immediate family members but hey that's another issue for another day, anyway I think it's time again for me to forcefully push myself back onto my neutral path again before I slip back onto the treadmill of self-destruction again, so for now it will be safe for me to be silent, reserved and go into my agoraphobic confinement where I do my best not to allow any unpleasant thoughts in my head to reignite.

I ought to be proud of myself that I am managing to keep the lid on it even though it gets extremely hard at times, but I don't want to give up searching for that light at the end of my tunnel.

July 30, 2020.

Worked three hours this morning doing my best to avoid negativities so that I can concentrate on building my courage and confidence and lift my spirits up, and in the afternoon seen the hand therapist, we spoke about me driving my manual vehicle and that I should still wear the splint on my left forearm for another four weeks and that he will speak with Miss X and work injury Doctor.

Apparently Miss X has been up to her old tricks again with my treaters to get me back to work before it's appropriate so that she can get her fat bonus from her firm and the insurer, the rest of day and night and even some days ahead I don't want to think or write anything negative if I can help it in order to get myself out of this predicament I'm in.

August 06, 2020.

Worked three hours again this morning, done the usual photo copying, scanning and counting of some products.

I could feel that my confidence levels were rising a bit so with that in mind I went and had a chat with the safety manager explaining to him that I am ready to increase my hours and soon get back to full time hours and back to full capacity, so he was happy with that I thought and when I got home I called the work injury Doctor and made her aware of my intentions and thankfully she was all for it and gave me a full capacity form so that as of Monday morning I can resume my full time position with my employer.

I received a phone call from my employers safety manager mid afternoon telling me to hold off for the moment that there's not enough work for me for eight hours every day with my restrictions and my forearm being in a splint, so I will find out tomorrow, there we go I am trying to lift my spirits up and make every effort to go back to work.

I'll be sitting here rest of the day and night wandering what hurdles will be thrown on my path to prolong the return to work progress, I'll just wait and see what the outcome is tomorrow.

I don't want it to worry me and I don't want it to heighten me, just want to be neutral.

August 7, 2020.

I've received that much anticipated phone call from my employers safety manager telling me that until the splint is removed from my left forearm and I'm close to driving a forklift that I should be on restricted hours and restricted duties, well I guess I had no other option but to agree.

I will speak with the hand therapist and the work injury Doctor today and tomorrow and I am ready to make a concerted effort to drive my manual vehicle, not long after I received a call from Miss X and almost the same conversation with her about return to work

We agreed that next week I'll go to work for three days and three hours each day until I sort it out with my treaters, I guess it is what it is I just need to go along with the implementations of my treaters, and it is imperative for me to put myself at a point of no return, I've travelled too far and too long in the dark to except bureaucratic bullshit, I'm starting to believe that I'm getting closer and closer to the end of this ordeal where I need to have my fulltime position back that it may somehow have a dictative element or an effect to get me out of my tunnel for good. I don't want to make any other comments except I just got to keep on jumping over the hurdles until I get myself on to a clear field.

August 10, 2020.

I've seen the work injury Doctor this morning for no reason other than getting a renewed capacity form so that I can continue performing light duties at my work place until I get clearances from all my medical professionals, anyhow back to work for another three hours today, it was just a usual attitude, the atmosphere was very dull, and I did my usual scanning of documents that could have been done in thirty minutes I had to drag it out to three hours

According to bureaucratic bullshit I have to be at my work place for those three hours, other ways I've been told bluntly that if I don't attend I will not receive weekly payments, things like these are not only a reminder but almost a constant confirmation that I will never be free from hurdles on my path to recovery, anyway from here on I will make a concerted effort to get all the appropriate clearances one way or another so that I can get back to work on full time basis.

I need to do this and do it now, I simply am so fearful of hitting the bottom again and if that happens I don't believe I would be so determent to get myself out of it, so it could be the end, as much as I wanted justice in a right manner in the court of law it didn't happen and as much as I am doing my best to deter my thoughts right away from retributive justice it really makes it hard when I get hurdles placed on my path time and time again.

This is the time the emotion that surrounds the idea of vengeance becomes an insatiable hunger for violent revenge that sets itself in the corners of my mind like concrete and it hardens itself and it becomes an impossible task to chisel it out of my head, but for now I need to ignore all this negative emotions if I am to make the prodigious decision to pick myself up of the ground dust off and concentrate on moving forward, this is where I need optimism and hopefulness, this would be the right time to cut ties with more negative people to keep me on my path to get me out of my darkness so that I can have the opportunity to move forward with some kind of positivity, well I might have mentioned it once or twice before that it is a very fine line between staying or leaving for good, without being unfair to the loyal people around me who are trying to help and encourage me to be normal again without understanding where I am and what I've been through but I do give them a lot of credit and a lot of respect.

Anyway, next few days I don't want to think of anything negative or positive I just want to be neutral, I just want to follow the instructions of the medical treaters and my employer to the best of my ability under the current circumstances, I guess I just want some time out, even if it's temporary.

Chapter 23

August 26, 2020.
Okay the last couple of weeks I didn't feel like writing anything, but I've been busy trying my hardest to get all the appropriate clearances so I can return to my usual task on a fulltime basis with my employer, even though mentally I'm not out of the woods and physically with my left shoulder and my left forearm I'm only able to use them between sixty to seventy percent for some reason I've managed to get the clearances.

My medical treaters ask me to rate my pain between one to ten and obviously they take my word for it good or bad and that's where it ends, anyhow after all the uphill battles obviously I want to cut long story short, well YES!!!

I've started my usual hours on fulltime basis, I thought yes maybe this is the time the heavily dimmed scrawny light at the end of my tunnel will become enlarged maybe this is the time it will be a lot brighter so I can have some indication of where I'm going maybe this is the time where the opportunity will present itself for me to regain some self respect, some happiness and some kind of normality, so I've started my day at six am with low level of optimism but by towards the end of my shift I could feel my optimism levels have lifted and I felt my spirits are starting to lift so I thought from here the next two to four weeks there would be no reason why I shouldn't be back to almost full normality.

Ten minutes before my shift ended I was called into my managers office to be told that as of tomorrow I should stay home and that I will get my weekly payment until my employer organizes one last independent medical examination, and when the results come back and it's all clear I will resume my fulltime position with the company.

When I left the manager's office WOW and WOW I thought, what the hell are they trying to do to me? I thought I had all the necessary clearances from all my medical treaters, so therefore I've cancelled all my appointments with the psychiatrist, the psychologist, the liaison lady, the hand therapist, the work injury doctor and the insurer thinking that I'm okay and it's safe for me to return to work.

I truly don't understand the purpose of this final IME to be organized by my employer, so not knowing and not understanding obviously prompted my blood to boil to the point where the anger levels are rising and the burning desires of inflicting pain and violence onto others are reigniting again, oh boy what do I do ? Where do I go? How do I act? How do I react?

Half way home I had to pull over on the side of the road, I can feel myself trembling with rage, so I sat in the car for almost an hour trying to calm myself down with countless cigarettes thinking and thinking that I should not and I will not take this home, my wife has seen enough and gone through enough of this bullshit, so once again I will forcefully put that fake smile on my face when I get home and tell my wife that everything is alright, for how long?

I don't know, anyway up until this afternoon thinking that I am taking the reins in my own hands and that my mental health and my physical well being is improving all good so about the middle of October I can use some of my long service leave and be with my daughter in Alice springs for the safe arrival of my first grandchild into this world, but now with this independent medical examination that's been unfairly enforced by my employer I don't know if my chance of being with my daughter is blown out the water, but for now I guess I have no option but to wait patiently without doing anything unreasonable that I might regret.

September 3, 2020.
Okay after a long anticipation, anxiousness and lots of heavy breathings I finally received an email with the date of medical examination the seventh of this month and they also informed me with dictatorial attitude that after the assessment until they take appropriate course of action I am to stay away from my employment work place and I am to refrain from communicating or corresponding with any of my work colleagues, clients or customers by any means either during or outside working hours either directly or through another person in relation to this matter.

Upon review of the result from the examiner they will arrange a time to meet with me to discuss my return to work plan, none of this makes sense while I'm trying to come out of my useless and worthless state that I've been in, and now I am made to feel like a criminal as well, and when I asked my employer Why?

I was told that it's a common practise, Just do it I have no choice. Oh by the way for this independent medical examination my employer have their own terminology calling it " functional capacity assessment" so without my employers realisation this is bringing me down and forcing me back into my agoraphobic confinement again.

Here I go again using a lot of my strength and powers to stay strong, I wish there was an easy way to make people understand how hard and how real this is. Anyway I just got to wait till this storm is over so that I can stop going around and around like a leaf.

September 7, 2020.
Finally the day for the last medical examination is here today

I've seen the examiner in Melbourne at seven forty five this morning, I've answered all his questions in a proper manner and even though the capacity of my left shoulder and my left forearm is reduced to between sixty to seventy percent I've done my best with the movements to convince the examiner that I'm okay.

Some of the movements he made me do did cause some degree of discomfort and started my shoulder to ache but I tried my hardest not to show it.

When I left I felt the examining went well and I am very hopeful that my employer will not come up with a new obstacle to prevent me from returning to work, as I said recently that I want some normality back in my life and I want to start going forward.

September 17, 2020.
Received a phone call from my manager yesterday at ten am telling me that the examiner's report was good and I was cleared to come back to work today on normal duties and normal hours

The first thing this morning I've had a brief conversation with my manager explaining to him that even though I have all the appropriate clearances and leading up to the very last clearance the agony I went through has made me very tired mentally and I would like to be in Alice Springs next month for the birth of my first grandchild, so I would like to have six weeks off of my long service leave effective immediately.

He wasn't overly happy with my request but for some reason he agreed for me to start from tomorrow, so I stayed at work today only to unload couple of trucks and put some new products in their places in the storage areas, no physical work and no pick and pack orders.

When I arrived home this afternoon all my attention turn to the prospect of me being with my daughter at the birth of my grandchild.

FINAL CHAPTER.

After a few days I arrived in Alice springs, my wife arrived one week earlier.

After the longest fourteen days of my life in quarantine then released, the next couple of weeks spending with our daughter and welcoming our first grandchild into this world, the first two weeks here in Alice springs in quarantine was hard but what made it a little easier for me is that I've already been in an agoraphobic state for a long time, so being locked up in isolation for two weeks didn't feel unusual at all.

When I arrived back in Melbourne I felt that I needed more time to consolidate my thoughts and increase the usage and strength on my left shoulder and my left forearm, so I've decided to email my manager requesting one more week off of my long service leave, but my request was bluntly rejected, so on the second of November 2021 I returned back to work, again there was a very cold reception

There was no interest in my mental wellbeing or my physical wellbeing at all, I was lucky to get hello from a couple of people, and as for my manager once again he told me that I am no longer a team leader and I shouldn't have nothing to do with the running of the loading bays and handed me some picking slips to pick and pack orders and load and unload trucks.

This went on for a few days my team members are avoiding me and most importantly the safety manager is doing his absolute best not to come near me, and further more to my dilemma one of my team member which I thought we were good friends that we had morning tea and lunch together for the last eleven years was distancing himself from me, wow.

I thought what a way to lift someone's spirits by welcoming a person back to work after a long rehabilitation and recovery, I actually felt downgraded, angry, sad and sorry for myself, then I started to think was I that much of a bad person? Have I done something so drastic? so terrible? that made my team members turn their backs on me.

I mean after all I was the injured one I was the one that was harassed and bullied, well this is not doing me any good in my mental department, if I thought I was getting out of my darkness is this going to be a good reason for me to start sinking towards the bottom again, and is this going to be a confirmation for me to except that I am useless and worthless again.

By now I can feel the levels of my anxiety rising but somehow I'm determined to keep the lid on and keep cool, anyway being heavily involved in my usual tasks of picking and packing orders and loading trucks with the capacity of about sixty percent usage of my left shoulder and left forearm that I think it was only natural that I was using my right arm over excessively so on the fourth and fifth day I could feel heavy pain setting deep into my right shoulder.

At first I thought I might have pulled a muscle and that it will go away in a few days, but that wasn't the case, I didn't report it to no one because no one's talking to me so therefore no one would be interested.

I kept working and putting up with the pain until the eleventh of January 2021 that's when I went and seen the work injury Doctor and from then on things started to go downhill again, and I thought here we go again déjà vu.

Cutting the long story short, it was a very similar ordeal to 2019 and 2020, so up until April 2021 back to work on light duties and the usual downgrading attitude from my colleagues, and on the 28th of April I had the surgery done on my right shoulder.

Not long after I started to have psychology sessions once a week again and then started physio sessions once a week again, while this is all happening I did not hear from anyone at my work place until the end of September, only the new safety manager contacted me and only because higher authority had issued a notice to my employer for not checking up on me, so yeah this has forced me to re-enter my darkness again, dark and dangerous thoughts again

In my head I'm entertaining contemplations and ideations again, then again on the other hand I'm thinking if I had some empathy some respect and some spirit lifting attitude from my colleagues at my work place maybe things might have been different, with my head the way it is at the moment.

Again I'm very short with people in fact early November 2021 I was almost escorted of the premises of a large building product retailer store by two security officers and I also chased a food delivery person away from my house for a reason that was not warranted for me to lose it so quickly and the relationship with my wife and my kids are on the downward slope that I'm not happy and not proud of.

So for the safety of others and the safety of myself I've declared to my medical treaters that I need to remove myself from all this before it gets out of hand so I took my wife to a secluded place where there will be no knocking on the door and no answering any phone calls.

It was only five days but it was appropriate and safe, anyway amongst all this it was scheduled for me to have a meeting with the safety manager at my work place on the 19th of January 2022 to discuss about me returning to work on suitable duties until I get all the necessary clearances to resume my fulltime tasks again sometime in the near future.

I received an email that the safety manager won't be in until the 24th of January, anyway while I'm still getting psychology sessions per week and physio once a week I've managed to go to work for the second time for two hours on the seventh of February 2022 what was meant to be admin work in the office knowing that I can't reach above my shoulder level and I can't be involved in repetitive activities and yet my manager has organized work for me in the warehouse picking up rubbish and sweeping the floors.

If that wasn't bad enough but maybe manageable what made it worse was seeing some of my colleagues driving past on their forklifts with smirk on their faces, that was downgrading and severely intimidating, when I arrived home I was heightened and very angry.

I felt that I needed to make some serious decisions and that I never wanted to go to my current work place never again, so on the tenth of February 2022 I felt compelled and somewhat dictated by my current mental situation and dire circumstances to resign and I did.

Now three weeks since I've resigned I've received a no life changing payment for my entitlements that were accumulated annual leave, long service leave and roster day leave, it was just transferred in to my account with no pay slip, no appreciation letter no farewell no nothing and I haven't heard from anyone that I've worked with for almost twelve years.

This was the right time for me to remove myself completely from all this, now there will be a small payment for pain and suffering and my current mental situation that I've been put into by the people who have no empathy, no respect and no understanding at my work place, and maybe there's a good chance that I will be free from being oppressed and ostracized by these people.

The way what I have experienced and learned to live with is that there are three positive elements that constantly pushes me close to the edge are being misheard, being misunderstood and being ignored, firstly being misheard is when I speak to some people I can see in their eyes that they are not listening and that they are preoccupied so they haven't heard a word I've said, secondly about being misunderstood I've spoken to some other people I've noticed that they are listening but in their minds they are too busy formulating an artificial knowledge turning it into an opinion to give it to me, and when they do they have done their job so therefore there's no reason for them to see me for at least six weeks, so thirdly that's when being ignored begins, being ignored can also be a confirmation that I'm not important enough, I'm not worthy enough and there's no value or reason for me to be alive.

These three elements are one of the main reasons why I've been pushed into an agoraphobic state involuntarily, however I'm more aware of these three elements now than before but I still don't have the power or the strength to deal with it appropriately, maybe one day I will.

It is now May 2023 due to constant pain on both my shoulders and my left forearm and my mental state still hasn't improved I still see the psychologist once a week and still see the physiologist once a week so therefore I still receive weekly payments from the insurer, so the ordeal is not over yet and I don't know when it will be.

Even though there's no immediate future plans and there's nothing on the horizon for the future employment prospect that it may allow me to take my time to think carefully and seriously to make one final decision as to which direction will I take. In order to minimize the weight of that final decision I feel the need to disappear into my own wilderness for some time, maybe weeks or even months where I can try to eliminate the dangerous thoughts and the ideations and further more the retributive justice like avenging fatal and final revenge, knowing that I'm not out of the woods yet and often I feel like I'm a ticking time bomb ready to explode at any moment at any situation.

I don't think I ever will be out of the woods based on the fear that the pilot light can reignite at any moment, and knowingly excepting that I will not be able to eliminate all my negative thoughts and emotions as quickly as I would like and it will take time and will be extremely hard to make the final decision on which path to walk on or not.

As much as I would like to complete these chapters stop writing and walk away completely from everything and most people that have become so insignificant to me but I just can't seem to walk away for good, simply because the misery continues, it is now mid February 2024 not much has changed nor is it changing.

Around August 2023, my psychologist strongly suggested that I get TMS treatment [Transcranial magnatic stimulation], once again I had to go through the right channels like getting a referral from the psychiatrist which takes weeks to receive and the approval from the insurer, again it takes weeks to receive.

Once all that was arranged I ended up spending three days and nights in a mental hospital in the western suburb of Melbourne and had one session of TMS treatment that had no effect or impact to my mental state.

I was there September 2023 Friday night, Saturday night and Sunday night, when Monday morning arrived I couldn't wait to get out of there, I've became so edgy and heightened almost to the maximum level that I've informed the hospital staff that if they don't release me officially I will jump over the fence and go home, but they've reluctantly agreed and after some phone conversations they've walked me out and left me in front of the hospital with no concern at al.

Maybe am one of the lucky ones to have the ability and somewhat capability to keep the lid on with extreme difficulty, it wasn't a good feeling what it felt like being thrown out of mental hospital and left on the foot path to fend for myself, however I've managed to get a taxi and get home safely.

It is now September 2024 I still believe that I'm not out of the woods yet and what makes me believe is that I constantly think and accept that my dignity is tarnished and my integrity is way down low where it almost feels that it is beyond repair and if the recovery mechanism does exist well it doesn't seem to be in sight for me at the moment but I will do my best to keep the lid on as tight as possible and for as long as possible.

I do believe this will all end one day but how? I will never know.

One of the reasons of me promulgating my deep, dark and raw moments of my life in the last nearly six years is not about winning or losing as it is not a trophy winning competition as such and that if anyone else is going through similar thoughts and emotions is that we're not alone and it is just a matter of me relying and depending on my patience and my inner strength to stay on the path of life willingly or unwillingly.

I strongly believe that there's no help from anyone or anything, so I will be doing my absolute best on my own and with powerful determination to deter myself away from reaching my destination involuntarily, if not for me I feel powerfully compelled to stay around a little longer for the ones I love so dearly.

THE END.

www.ingramcontent.com/pod-product-compliance
Lightning Source LLC
Chambersburg PA
CBHW030035100526
44590CB00011B/214